CHRIST
in My Career

Allen W. Graves

Convention Press

NASHVILLE   TENNESSEE

Printed in the United States of America
70. MY 57 R.R.D.

ABOUT THE AUTHOR

ALLEN W. GRAVES is dean of the School of Religious Education of the Southern Baptist Theological Seminary, Louisville, Kentucky. He went to the seminary in 1955 from the pastorate of the Immanuel Baptist Church in Tulsa, Oklahoma. Previous pastorates were at First Baptist Church of Charlottesville, Virginia; First Baptist Church of Fort Pierce, Florida; student pastorates in Kentucky and Illinois.

From 1941-1943 he was director of Young People's work in the Training Union Department of the Baptist Sunday School Board, Nashville, Tennessee.

Dr. Graves was born near Rector, Arkansas. The family soon moved to southern Illinois where he received his elementary, high school, and college training. After graduating from Southern Illinois University at Carbondale, he taught school in his home town of Herrin, Illinois, and pastored rural churches. He entered Southern Baptist Theological Seminary in 1936 and graduated with the Th.M. degree in 1939 and the Th.D. degree in 1942. He was married in 1937 to Helen Cannan who was the Baptist Student Union secretary for Southern Illinois University. They have six children.

Dr. Graves has served as author of curriculum materials for Sunday school and Training Union, as a member of the Southern Baptist Radio and Television Commission, and as chairman of a special committee on church-related vocations appointed by the Southern Baptist Convention in 1956.

iii

ACKNOWLEDGMENTS

Grateful acknowledgment is made to the following publishers and authors for the use of copyrighted material in this book:

Abingdon Press for selections from *Careers for You,* by Erma Paul Ferrari.

Friendship Press for material from *There's a Job for You,* by Ruth Ransom.

Harper and Brothers for a quotation from *Your Other Vocation,* by Elton Trueblood.

CONTENTS

v

CHAPTER 1 OUTLINE

I. THE CHRISTIAN BELONGS TO GOD
1. The Christian's Talents Belong to God
2. Time Is to Be Used for God
3. Influence Belongs to God
4. Material Possessions Belong to God
5. Vocation Belongs to God

II. WHAT CAN BE DONE WITH A LIFE?

III. GOD HAS A PLAN
1. Every Christian in "Full-time Service"
2. Special Abilities Can Be Used

IV. CHOOSING GOD'S WAY OR MAN'S WAY
1. Determining Life's Aim
2. Giving God Priority

V. LIFE'S GREAT DECISIONS
1. Used of God
2. Joy and Greatness Through Service

VI. MAKING THE DECISION NOW
1. How God Guides
2. Each One Must Decide

1

All of Life Belongs to God

THE sales manager said, "Go out and get the business, whatever it takes! Drink with them, take them to the night clubs. Give the customers what they want if you want to get to the top." "If that's what it takes," said the ambitious young salesman, "then that is what I'll do, for I'm heading for the top."

"God hasn't called me to be a preacher, so I suppose that whatever I decide to do is up to me," a young man remarked in his Young People's union in a program on making one's vocation Christian.

"Well, I am just a homemaker," a young wife and mother said in her Sunday school class. "I don't suppose this discussion of making our vocations Christian applies to me."

What is wrong with these statements? Should a Christian "sell out on God" in order to achieve financial success? Is God interested in the vocational choices of preachers only?

Paul wrote, "What? know ye not that your body is the temple of the Holy Ghost which is in you, which ye have of God, and ye are not your own? For ye are bought with a price" (1 Cor. 6:19–20). Christians belong to God. A Christian's life is measured by the way in which it is used for God.

In Romans 12 : 4–5 and Ephesians 4 : 15–16 Paul speaks of the church as the body of Christ. In this body every part has its function, with Christ, the head, supplying the vital power and cohesive force.

The freedom of the Christian is disciplined by his loyalty to Christ and a desire to please him.

I. THE CHRISTIAN BELONGS TO GOD

1. *The Christian's Talents Belong to God*

One's talents have been entrusted to him with the confident expectation that he will develop them and use them in God's service. A keen mind, musical skill, ability as a speaker, and leadership ability are all gifts of God that the Christian will use as God may direct.

A young doctor prepared himself for medical missions in China. When the doors of opportunity closed there after World War II he practiced medicine in his home state. As a pediatrician he ministers with Christian love to the bodies and souls of children. Every week he is busy preaching, witnessing, and teaching in his church, a mission point, or in some other place of service. He uses his medical skill, his speaking ability, and his knowledge of the Bible in loving service for the Lord.

Paul's plea to the Christians at Rome is valid for every Christian young person today: "I beseech you therefore, brethren, by the mercies of God, that ye present your bodies a living sacrifice, holy, acceptable unto God, which is your reasonable service" (Rom. 12:1).

The minds, the bodies, and the skills of every Christian are to be used for God, for they were given by God to be used in the service of mankind.

2. Time Is to Be Used for God

The way in which a Christian uses his time will determine his success or failure in Christian living. No Christian has a right to "kill" time. Time is a precious gift from God to be invested wisely.

The proper use of time would solve the problems of many troubled and frustrated people. It would greatly reduce the difficulties experienced in the work of many churches.

The right use of time could bring education to the unlearned, prosperity to the poor, culture to the uncouth, and achievement to the discouraged.

Paul urges Christians to "walk in wisdom . . . , redeeming the time" (Col. 4:5). Ecclesiastes reminds every young person that "a wise man's heart discerneth both time and judgment" (Eccl. 8:5).

3. Influence Belongs to God

One can use his influence to draw others to Christ or he can use it to drive them away. One's example may lead others to seek the Saviour who can transform life. Or it may cause an unbeliever to lose all confidence in Christians.

Some people who never read the Bible, attend Sunday school, or hear a sermon can be greatly influenced by the life and testimony of a Christian. The life of a faithful Christian witness is an open book whose contents are obvious to all with whom he associates. Such a life is an unanswerable argument as to the reality of the saving and transforming power of Christ.

Every Christian wields an influence of some kind,

either good or bad. He either represents or misrepresents Jesus by the way he lives, works, talks, and worships. The right use of influence is a responsibility that every young Christian should welcome.

Paul advised, "For none of us liveth to himself, . . . It is good neither to eat flesh (meat offered to idols), not to drink wine, nor any thing whereby thy brother stumbleth, or is offended, or is made weak" (Rom. 14:7, 21).

4. Material Possessions Belong to God

Whatever God has entrusted to one's care he expects to be used for his glory. One acknowledges his stewardship by bringing to the Lord at least a tenth of all his possessions and demonstrates his love by giving liberally beyond the tithe.

God and man are partners in using material possessions. Man is responsible to God for an accounting of the material possessions entrusted to his care. The giving of the tenth to God does not invalidate God's claim upon the nine-tenths or upon all of the life of the Christian.

"The earth is the Lord's, and the fulness thereof; the world, and they that dwell therein" (Psalm 24:1).

"Every beast of the forest is mine, and the cattle upon a thousand hills" (Psalm 50:10). God claims title to the whole earth. Since all belongs to God, then the Christian should seek to use all he has in keeping with God's purposes and plans.

5. Vocation Belongs to God

Because the Christian belongs to God, he must seek God's direction in the investment of his life. He has no right to make his own decision about how his life shall be spent without consulting God, the owner. He who created and redeemed the Christian knows his life and his potentiality as no one else can. Therefore, to find the fullest possible enjoyment and achievement the sincere Christian must seek his guidance every step of the way.

Paul urged his fellow Christians to "walk worthy of the vocation wherewith ye are called, with all lowliness and meekness" (Eph. 4:1-2).

When a person becomes a Christian his whole life is committed to Christ as Lord. Christ bids his followers, "Thou shalt love the Lord thy God with all thy heart, and with all thy soul, and with all thy mind, and with all thy strength" (Mark 12:30). This demands that every Christian must serve God through his daily work. For most people the major concern of life is the work in which they are engaged from day to day. If this main stream of life is not dedicated to God and channeled into Christian service then that life is missing God's high purpose and ideal. Elton Trueblood, in his splendid book *Your Other Vocation,* has said, "The chief glory of work lies in the fact that it is really the only thing we can give that is our own." [1]

Professor Trueblood rejoices in "the growing awareness, on the part of those touched by the Christian gospel, of the meaning of vocation. The idea is that God can call us to many kinds of activity and that secular work well done is a holy enterprise. We have reacted violently, and with good reason, against the medieval heresy to the

[1] Elton Trueblood, *Your Other Vocation* (New York: Harper & Brothers, 1952) p. 61.

effect that there are religious levels, with common work in the world appearing at the bottom. Once many believed that it was best to be one of 'the religious,' associated with some monastic order, that it was second best to be a secular priest, and that it was third best to be an ordinary workman. Most of us now see this conception as a monstrous distortion of Christian truth, but it is still necessary to struggle against vestiges of it." [2]

One cannot commit his work to God until he has committed his life to him. For every Christian, life is a sacred trust from God. The Christian is responsible to God for the way he uses the life which God has entrusted to him.

The Christian layman, whether businessman, farmer, sociologist, or biologist is under the same obligation to measure up to the Christian standard of service and of moral and ethical behavior usually expected of the pastor or missionary. Each must measure his life by the same tests: Am I working for my own comfort, prestige, power, and glory, or am I dedicating my work to the benefit of mankind and the realization of Christ's purposes for man?

Every Christian must be willing to put God first, to say sincerely to God in every area of life, "Not my will, but thine, be done" (Luke 22:42).

II. What Can Be Done with a Life?

Every young Christian faces at some time the question, What shall I do with my life? Confusing ambitions and appeals draw him first this way, then that. He recog-

[2] *Ibid.*, p. 58.

nizes that many vocations are unworthy of a Christian and do not offer a challenging opportunity for the wisest use of the talents with which he has been divinely endowed. The young Christian finds himself asking, What can I do that is really worth while with my life? Where is my life needed most? What satisfactions may be gained through such a lifework? Where does God want me to serve?

The career of a present-day surgeon-anesthetist illustrates what a Christian can do with his life. As a young student he worked his way through a state university in the most difficult years of the depression. He was active in campus affairs, such as the medical honor society, dramatics, and the staff of the college paper. He was a loyal and effective member of the First Baptist Church and was elected by his fellow students as Baptist Student Union president on his campus and in the state organization.

His college pastor described the experience of this young college student concerning his vocation: "His great decision came in my study. The high calling in Christ Jesus came before him, and spiritual voices called in tender tones. Doors of opportunity opened in his vision. A great test comes to those who surrender completely to the authority of Christ and are willing to follow the Holy Spirit's leadership; but as we prayed together the answer came. He said: 'God has made his will clear to me. This day I know that God wants me to use my talents to help lift the crushing burdens and ease the pain and sorrow of humanity through the medical profession.'"

III. GOD HAS A PLAN

God has a plan for every life. A Christian's first responsibility is to find and follow that plan. The use of aptitude tests, surveys, and other such counseling aids must always be secondary to the larger decision to place one's life in the hands of God to do what he wants done, when he wants it, and wherever he may direct. Then the Christian can sing sincerely,

> I'll go where you want me to go, dear Lord
> O'er mountain or plain or sea;
> I'll say what you want me to say, dear Lord,
> I'll be what you want me to be.
> —MARY BROWN

1. *Every Christian in "Full-time Service"*

Baptist layman John J. Hurt, Jr., urges young people to "look again and more fully at John 15:16, 'Ye have not chosen me, but I have chosen you, and ordained you, that ye should go and bring forth fruit, and that your fruit should remain: that whatsoever ye shall ask of the Father in my name, he may give it you.'

"There is no escape in those words. Every Christian is ordained or set apart, to win others to Christ. There is failure unless the Christian life is totally committed to him. They watch the example more than they listen to the words. . . .

"We tamper with the message of the New Testament in this day when we refer to one dedicating himself to preaching or the like as 'answering the call to full-time Christian service.' We need Christian laymen just as we need ministers, and the call to both is for full-time Christian service. . . . It is the assignment for every Christian, whether he be a plumber or a preacher, a doctor or a director of religious activities, a mother in the home or a missionary in a foreign land. Christ has called. We are committed." [3]

Every Christian is obligated to find God's will for his life. No life is complete that neglects to honor God in daily work. Many people mistakenly assume that God is interested only in those Christians who are called into church-related vocations. God has a plan for every life. He wants to help those who enter every vocation to make theirs a Christian vocation and a means of accomplishing his way and his will in the world.

2. Special Abilities Can Be Used

Christian young people may fill some of the many opportunities for Christian service in government abroad. Each year the United States Foreign Service recruits approximately two hundred and fifty young men and young women to join the three thousand officers already in the Foreign Service Officer Corps who staff the American embassies, legations, and consulates throughout the world. Entrance to the foreign service is based upon written examination in English expression, general background, and modern languages. Further information concerning these examinations may be obtained from the Board of Examiners for the Foreign Service, Department of State, Washington 25, D. C.

The Christian who serves overseas, whether in some government agency, in military service, or as the com-

---

[3] John J. Hurt, Jr., *The Baptist Training Union Magazine,* March, 1957, p. 7.

mercial representative of some business corporation will find many opportunities for Christian witnessing. Christian love exemplified in the way one lives, in the way one worships, and the way one engages in social activities will demonstrate the vitality of his Christian faith. Such demonstrations will provide opportunities for bearing a vital witness to those in other lands who need Jesus as Saviour.

Here in the homeland also special abilities can be used effectively by the sincere Christian who would witness through every available opportunity.

A number of outstanding athletes have formed the Fellowship of Christian Athletes, Incorporated. An ace pitcher for the Philadelphia Phillies, in giving his testimony to a Baptist Brotherhood athletic banquet said: "We don't preach or anything like that. We're just a bunch of guys who believe in God and think Christianity is a good thing for us and our families. . . . If we as athletes can be an example to look up to for what we do on the playing field, then we can be an example to you because we believe in God and the Christian way of life."

Another member of the group is considered one of the finest *T* formation quarterbacks in all football history. Formerly with the Cleveland Browns, he threw 1,943 passes during his professional career and completed 1,057 of them, scoring 137 touchdowns through passing. In his testimony he emphasized: "You have to work at being a Christian and live it every day of your life. That doesn't mean you have to go to church seven days a week. You can be a good Christian on the football field, in the classroom, or in your business."

IV. Choosing God's Way or Man's Way

Every person has one life to live. How shall it be invested? If life is to be worth living, it must be lived for things of abiding value. It must have aims and goals that are worthy. Merely to have a good income, to be popular and prosperous, is not sufficient for a Christian.

What are the abiding values in life? For some, the chief goal in life is the respect, the companionship, and the affection of friends; for others, it is the love and fellowship that characterize a Christian home. All seek that inner joy that comes from helping those in need, the inner glow that comes when one has helped lift another's burden. One of the greatest joys in life is to bring others to know the redeeming love and continuing fellowship of Jesus Christ our Saviour.

1. *Determining Life's Aim*

Every Christian needs a clear and well-defined aim and purpose in life. As a self-testing exercise, write out the answers to the following questions: What are my life goals? What am I seeking from life? How do I expect to achieve my goal and purpose in life? What kind of a life do I expect to live? What kind of a person do I want to become? How am I preparing my life to reach that goal? What will the vocation I am considering do for me, for others, for God?

It is essential that one have some purpose in life before he can be successful. If one is able to give some clear statement of his overall purpose and goal in life he can then determine whether or not he is closer toward the goal he has set.

2. *Giving God Priority*

The beginning point for the Christian is recognizing the priority of God. Because the Christian belongs to God, he must seek God's will and his direction before making decisions as to the investment of his life, the choice of his career, the selection of his life companion, and the choice of his friends.

The determining of priorities in life is of great importance. Nothing is trivial in a matter so significant as this. That which may appear to be of little consequence in a person's life today will often become the most important factor tomorrow.

Many young Americans are more concerned about things to live with than they are about things to live for. Many are more concerned about automobiles, appliances, and laborsaving devices that provide luxurious living than they are with goals and purposes that make life worth while.

V. LIFE'S GREAT DECISIONS

Life's greatest joys are to be found in a meaningful religious faith, a happy marriage, and a satisfying, worthwhile vocation. Before reaching the age of twenty-five, most young Christians will probably have made definite decisions in all three of these areas. In none of them should a decision be made without God's leadership.

1. *Used of God*

Because the Christian's life belongs to God, he has dedicated his mind, his strength, his will, his all to Christ, to be used in his service.

There may be some individuals who resent the idea of being "used" by anyone. They may say they want no one to exploit them or take advantage of them. But when the Christian submits his life to Christ he finds not exploitation but the greatest possible fulfilment of self.

2. Joy and Greatness Through Service

Christ has declared the principles of true greatness and demonstrated them in his own life. "But he that is greatest among you, let him be as the younger; and he that is chief, as he that doth serve" (Luke 22:26).

The proof of a Christian's love is to be found in his obedient service. Jesus said, "Not every one that saith unto me, Lord, Lord, shall enter into the kingdom of heaven; but he that doeth the will of my Father which is in heaven" (Matt 7:21).

If one wants the greatest satisfaction from life he will willingly give and serve rather than receive and demand.

VI. Making the Decision Now

1. How God Guides

God's will for one's life may be revealed in many different ways. For one, the call may come suddenly, clearly, and unmistakably. For another, God's way may be revealed through the gradual awareness of a need which could be met by a talent which that person possesses. One should not expect to see his whole life mapped out plainly. God often reveals his will one step at a time. God wants his follower to use his mind, emotions, interests, and an objective survey of his abilities in finding his place of service.

When one places his life in God's hands to do only what he wills, he finds that God will guide him in discovering his talents and the opportunities for service where his life can be most useful. God will open the doors he wants his followers to enter if they ask, seek, and knock. God will close the doors one ought not enter as he did for Paul when he was calling him to Macedonia. In Acts 16:6–7, it is recorded that Paul and Silas were "forbidden of the Holy Ghost to preach the word in Asia," and that when they wanted to go to Bithynia "the Spirit suffered them not."

Like many a frustrated young person, Paul may have been wondering, "Lord, what do you want me to do?" But the Lord had a plan which was soon revealed, a call to Macedonia.

2. Each One Must Decide

In finding one's vocation, as in accepting Christ as Saviour, God does not force his will upon anyone. God knows each Christian personally and knows what is the best vocation for each life. But he has given to every man a free will. Because God has made man free to choose, it is possible for man to resist God's love and to reject his plan. Although God calls, man may fail to follow.

God expects every Christian to use his mind under the leadership of the Holy Spirit to discover all that he can about various fields of service and to learn what abilities and equipment he may have for effective service in each vocational field. God is ready to supply guidance and the Christian will be much in prayer as he seeks to find his place of vocational service.

Many young Christians will have received from their homes concepts of worth-while vocations. In school one may secure specific information about vocations and one's aptitudes for them. Friends are available for counsel. Literature is available, including the Bible which tells how God has dealt with other persons with similar problems. Many helpful books which deal with various vocations are available to help in understanding God's purposes for his people. Intelligence tests, aptitude tests, the counsel of friends and advisors, the information that comes from reading the Bible, and the inner leading of the Holy Spirit, all combine to help one find God's will. But the final choice of following or rejecting God's plan is up to each individual.

God has created and redeemed each Christian and each belongs to him. Yet God leaves to each individual the decision as to whether he will follow God's purpose for his life in Christian service.

TOPICS FOR FURTHER DISCUSSION

1. How often should a call be issued in church worship services for life dedication to church-related vocations?
2. How many churches in the association are seeking pastors, educational or church music workers, church secretaries, or other staff members?
3. Make a list of all those who have gone from the church into church-related vocations either at home or abroad.

CHAPTER 2 OUTLINE

I. GOD CALLS
1. What God Expects
2. Developing a Christian Concept of Vocation
3. The Scriptures Speak

II. ALL ARE CALLED
1. Is There a Difference in Calls?
2. God's Call to Church-related Vocations
3. Recognizing the Call of God
4. What Constitutes a Call?
5. No Standard Pattern

III. HOW SHOULD ONE RESPOND?
1. God's Prior Claim
2. Consider Needs
3. Influence of Home and Church
4. A Personal Decision

IV. RE-EXAMINING VOCATIONAL CHOICES
1. Remedying Wrong Choices
2. Recapturing Ideals and Dreams
3. A Call to Change Vocations
4. These Made the Change
5. More Information Encourages New Decisions

V. BEING CHRISTIAN IN EVERY VOCATION
1. The Christian Way Is the Happiest Way
2. God's Way Is the Surest Way
3. Christ's Way Is a Fruitful Way
4. Christ's Way a Way of Sacrifice and Service

2

All Are Called

Has God given "to every man his work"? (Mark 13:34). Can all vocations be Christian vocations? What vocations offer possibilities for Christian people for a lifetime of dedicated service? How can a person set Christian standards for the choice of a vocation? Does God call men into the fields of medicine, law, teaching, agriculture, as he calls men into the preaching ministry, the ministry of religious education, or the ministry of church music? If one wants to serve God, must he do only "church work"?

If these questions have been cause for concern, this chapter should be helpful.

I. God Calls

Baptists have always believed in a God-called ministry. Most of those who have offered themselves for service in church-related vocations have done so in response to an inner leading of the Holy Spirit. It is generally expected that church staff members and denominational workers should be called of God to their tasks. But what is often overlooked is that God has a plan and a purpose for every Christian and will direct each individual into the place of service he has for him.

17

1. *What God Expects*

There are certain things that God expects of every Christian everywhere. Everyone is called first of all to forsake sin and to follow Christ. This decision to follow Christ means that every day a Christian's acts, words, and attitudes will show that Christ is in control. As a Christian he is to live in obedience to God's divine leadership each step of the way. He will think first about what God wants him to do and will strive to follow daily the principles of love, righteousness, and unselfishness that Jesus taught and lived.

This means that God is not only keenly interested in the vocational choice of every Christian, but also that he is ready to make his will known to all followers who seek his direction. Just as many Christians have had a clear and definite call into the ministry so many others have felt clear leadership from the Lord to enter the fields of medicine, art, literature, social work, or politics.

The poet William Wordsworth felt an indescribable necessity laid upon him to be an interpreter to all men of the beauty of nature. Sculptors and musicians have given testimony to their feeling of direct guidance from the Lord in the pursuit of their professions. Certainly God needs men and women in every area of the world's work.

God calls. The faithful Christian will seek to follow where he leads.

2. *Developing a Christian Concept of Vocation*

Following God's purpose for one's life is not always easy because of the complicated structure of modern society and the division of occupations into the hundreds of highly specialized vocations through which young people may serve.

Yet, in the finding of a career, the Christian is concerned that he will be guided by Christian considerations at every point. Work is one of the basic concerns of every life. And a vital religion will be inseparably bound up not only with the seeking of a vocation but also with the pursuing of that vocation throughout life.

It is unfortunate when any Christian attempts to separate his religion from his daily work.

(1) *Attitude of business and government.*—Business and industry have in recent decades been attempting to overcome the tragic mistakes made during the past century in their interpretation of work.

Since the beginning of the industrial revolution, industrialists assumed that their employees looked upon work as a painful and unpleasant necessity to be endured by the worker only to enable him to secure the good things in life which work made possible. Labor policies were then determined with the idea that fear of starvation was the main incentive to work and that in order to secure more work or a better quality of work the employer must increase the rate of pay.

When the government removed the fear of starvation by various forms of welfare state planning, the industrialists sought for other means of persuading their employees to take a real interest in their work. Out of this process came welfare programs, paid holidays, recreational programs, free medical treatment, and other means of satisfying the physical needs of the workers.

Only in recent years have leaders in business and industry realized that they have overlooked the psychological needs of their employees. They failed to appeal to their sense of responsibility, their pride of craft, their self-respect, their sense of social usefulness and community status. Employers are learning that their employees want to feel accepted, that their work is worth while, and that the community looks upon them with approval.

Churches can make a real contribution to people by helping them to have a Christian viewpoint of work.

(2) *Three views of work.*—A classic illustration of the varying viewpoints of work is given in the inquiry made of three men engaged in the construction of a cathedral. The first, when asked "What are you doing?" replied, "I'm earning two dollars an hour." The second answered, "I'm carrying bricks." The third replied, "I'm helping build a cathedral."

Every Christian needs to see his daily work as a significant contribution to the ongoing of God's world. When this is not so, work can be miserable drudgery.

(3) *Right motives for work.*—Since it is the normal thing for all of the men and a great many of the women in the United States to find a job and go to work when they have completed their education, it is important that they take this step with the right motivation.

Some people work only because of the economic pressures that make it necessary for them to have an income. Food, clothing, shelter, medical care, and other expenses require an income and therefore they must find employment to provide their economic necessities.

Christian young people, however, will approach their vocational work on the basis of loftier motives than these. The Christian rejects the view of work which looks upon it as the antithesis of all pleasure and happiness. The Christian does not look at the hours spent on his job as so much time taken from his real life and sold to his employer in return for the privilege of being able to live the rest of his life as he may choose. Work for the Christian is something performed for the glory of God and is a means of expressing his stewardship.

It would be an interesting experiment to interview several people who are engaged in different types of work. Each may be asked if he looks upon his work as a means of serving God and how he attempts to honor Christ through his vocation.

A Christian must often decide his own personal course of conduct when a decision of his labor union, of the chamber of commerce, or of an officer of his company conflicts with his Christian convictions.

Being a Christian in one's vocation involves more than just giving a day's work for a day's pay. One's religion must be demonstrated in every aspect of his work.

3. *The Scriptures Speak*

Paul declares that there is no circumstance of life in which the Christian cannot be faithful to God. Every honorable vocation can be used of God. After discussing slavery and freedom, Paul writes, "My brothers, let every one of us continue to live his life with God in the state in which he was when he was called" (1 Cor. 7:24 Phillips). Whether in the factory or front office, in the kitchen or the schoolroom, the Christian will be able to make of his work a service to God. Each one can faithfully witness for Christ in the place where he is, empowered and inspired by the indwelling Spirit of God.

The author of Hebrews addresses all of his Christian readers, "Wherefore, holy brethren, partakers of the heavenly calling . . ." (Heb. 3:1). Every true Christian is separated unto the service of God.

Paul expresses this same idea when he writes to Timothy of the God "who hath saved us, and called us with an holy calling, not according to our works, but according to his own purpose and grace" (2 Tim. 1:9).

II. ALL ARE CALLED

1. *Is There a Difference in Calls?*

How is the minister's call different from that of his faithful deacon who is a farmer or a lawyer?

The prevailing attitude among many Christians is that there are three types of vocations: "sacred"—including the church-related vocations; permissible or acceptable "secular" vocations; and forbidden vocations, such as the manufacture or sale of alcoholic beverages, gambling, etc., in which no Christian should engage.

Is this viewpoint scripturally sound? Is it proper to exhalt a call to the mission field as a higher calling than the call of God to another place of sacrificial service?

All Christians are called to a life of commitment, to a life of service to Christ and to their fellow men. The "highest call" for any Christian is to the place of service in which God wants him. Some will render that service through a church-related vocation. Others will render service equally acceptable in some "lay" occupation.

Realizing these facts will keep one from a false distinction between the secular and the sacred. Christians are always and everywhere responsible to God.

Unfortunately, this sense of a divine call is often very faint or entirely lacking in Christians earning their living in lay occupations. But for those entering church-related vocations there has been always the insistence upon their feeling that their decision comes as a direct and definite response to God's call.

2. God's Call to Church-related Vocations

A sense of call should not be excluded in other occupations, and certainly it should always be present in church-related vocations. Such a call need not be dramatic or spectacular. It usually is not, but it will bring a sense of mission. It often comes about with the recognition of a real need to be met, a realization that God has given the ability and the aptitudes to meet the need, and a willingness on the part of the Christian to give his life in helping to meet that need.

Most mature, useful Christian pastors, missionaries, or other church workers report that their calls were not particularly dramatic. They heard no audible voices, saw no visions in the sky. They gradually came to the conviction that service in some church-related vocations was God's plan for their lives. Some will admit that they postponed an immediate response to God's plan but, as the conviction grew stronger that God was calling them, they found happiness and spiritual strength in yielding their lives to the leadership of God. No one should enter a church-related vocation without this conviction.

3. Recognizing the Call of God

How can a Christian recognize the call of God? When God wants one to serve him in a church-related vocation or in some other vocation how does he let one know? What constitutes a divine call?

Some have assumed that every call to service comes like that of Isaiah or that of Paul, but many testify that God called them, not through some sudden, cataclysmic experience but through the quiet inner leading of the Spirit over a period of many months, perhaps years. Discovering one's lifework may be a process covering many years.

Whether God is calling to a "secular" or a church-related vocation, the Christian can know God's will by earnest prayer. When a Christian seeks the leadership and enlightenment of the Holy Spirit, he always finds the help he needs. Jesus promised that the Holy Spirit would guide "into all truth" (John 16 : 13–15).

James in his epistle urged, "If any of you lack wisdom, let him ask of God, that giveth to all men liberally, and upbraideth not; and it shall be given him" (James 1 : 5).

4. *What Constitutes a Call?*

There may be several elements in a call to any vocation. Always there is the call to be a Christian, to follow Jesus. Then there is that inner persuasion or conviction that one is being directly summoned to take up some vocation in which he can render Christian service. God indicates his will for one's life by equipping him with the talents necessary for such Christian service and by guiding him providentially in life's circumstances to make such service possible.

Another evidence of a divine call is found in the opening of doors of opportunity, as by the action of a church or denominational agency or some business firm. When

God leads a church to extend a call to a person to perform a spiritual ministry, such divine direction should certainly be considered as another way in which God makes his will known.

A call from God may or may not be accompanied by emotional elements, but certainly one's decision ought to involve one's will and emotional consent as well as the assent of his mind and logical reasoning.

5. No Standard Pattern

One should certainly beware of attempting to demand a standardized pattern of God's methods in dealing with men. God will call in the way that is most fitting. He will make the approach that seems wisest to him. God is much more likely to use the normal channels of one's own mental processes and emotional responses than to give directions by heavenly visions or audible voices in space. God speaks through ordinary events just as clearly and profoundly as through extraordinary events.

God expects one to study his own abilities and the needs of the world about him. One should be in such constant touch with God that when God speaks concerning his will for one's life, there will be instant readiness to respond to his call. That call may come suddenly and with great emotional upheaval or it may come quietly and over a much longer period.

In a survey made among 477 foreign missionaries, Dr. Winston Crawley reported that 73 per cent had a gradual call, while 27 per cent felt the call suddenly.

At the time of the call, one may not be conscious that the Holy Spirit is leading to a particular vocation. After the end of a long process, one may be able to look back over his experience and recognize that God has been leading in the events that have directed him to his vocation.

"God will speak to you according to your own temperament and personality, and he will speak again and again. Finding his will for your life is not one single act. You must keep listening for his guidance, which comes through prayer, Bible reading, and meditation; through the words of those who know his way and those who can point out the needs of the world; through daily experiences in tasks at hand in which you use all the personality, skill, determination, and love that God has given you." [1]

III. How Should One Respond?

1. *God's Prior Claim*

Every individual should turn from sin, accept Christ as Saviour, and confess him before men. Everyone should dedicate all of his life to Christ as Lord. Having done so, he will be concerned to find the place where he can best serve the Lord. It is at this point that every Christian should give prayerful consideration to church-related vocations along with his consideration of lay or "secular" employment.

2. *Consider Needs*

When one sees the needs of a sinful world, he recognizes that nothing is quite so urgent and so important as

[1] Ruth Ransom, *There's a Job for You* (New York: Friendship Press, 1946), p. 7.

the mission of bringing Christ to those in need. The Christian will see those needs and recognize his responsibility for meeting them because of his relationship with God and his desire to share his love with others. One is then in a position to respond to God's leading into that vocation where he can serve best.

3. *Influence of Home and Church*

The realization of the way in which God may desire one to serve him may come very early, particularly when one has a godly home with parents who pray that their children will respond to the leadership of God. Fortunate indeed are those young people who have fathers and mothers who rejoice to see their children going into Christian service in some church-related vocation or some vital vocation with Christian opportunities.

The influence of the church and its leaders may be the most important factor in helping other young people make these decisions. The personal example of the dedicated preacher, minister of music, or another church worker, whether on the paid church staff or a volunteer teacher or leader, may be the determining factor in helping a young person to find God's will. Evangelists, as they preach and extend the invitation, are often used of God in presenting the claims of Christ and leading young people to respond to the will of God concerning their vocations.

Many young people hear God's call to a particular field of service while attending some church assembly, convention, or camp. In the environment of careful study of various vocations and in the atmosphere of life dedication that usually characterizes such youth conferences, many young people answer the call that determines their vocational destiny.

4. A Personal Decision

Regardless of the assistance, encouragement, and information that may come from parents, church leaders, friends, and other sources, ultimately the individual must make his own decision concerning his response to God's call. God has given to each one the privilege and the responsibility of choosing his own way or God's way. The answering of the call of God must be a deliberate, thoughtful, and personal response to the question, What is God's will for me? This decision must be intensely personal. It is one that no one else can or should make. Yet it is one that each individual can make properly only if he has adequate information about himself and the needs of the world and an understanding of the Christian concept of vocation.

IV. RE-EXAMINING VOCATIONAL CHOICES

1. Remedying Wrong Choices

One who has not followed God's leadership vocationally is sometimes described as a "square peg in a round hole." Millions of people have drifted into vocations for which they feel no enthusiasm. For them the future is an uninviting round of drudgery and duty! Youthful dreams fade as they find themselves doing that which can never bring happiness and satisfaction.

To enter or continue in a vocation for which one is not suited may bring serious emotional problems.

One young person who had developed great skill as an artist was forced by his father to enter another profession which he disliked thoroughly and for which he had no aptitude. Under the frustrating pressure of such circumstances he soon became the victim of a mental disorder.

The large number of vocations available to young people today may seem to make the lifework decision complex and confusing. However, practically everyone willing to make the necessary effort can find the job that will be exactly the right one.

There is no need to endure the frustration of being a "square peg in a round hole" when so much help is available in finding the right vocation. Some have used the process of job experimentation to find the right place. A better plan would be to make a more careful investigation of one's abilities under God's guidance and make adequate preparation for the right job from the beginning.

2. Recapturing Ideals and Dreams

Once motivated by high ideals and noble purposes as adolescents, some young people have yielded to the alluring prospect of high wages and luxuries and turned aside from their original vocational impressions. Some drop out of the educational program that would prepare them for effective and worth-while service to their fellow men.

How shall young people get back on the right track when they feel that they have taken the wrong turn in the past? Shall the young television repairman sell his shop and tools and struggle through engineering school to become the electrical engineer he has always hoped and dreamed to be? Shall the young accountant on the way up leave behind his favorable business connections to enter a school of religious education to prepare to serve some church as a minister of education? Shall the young man who dreamed of being a doctor be content to be a drug store clerk?

3. *A Call to Change Vocations*

Within a given field there are vast possibilities for growth and increased responsibility. A change in the type of work done may come about as a result of faithful work in one's present vocation. Promotion may mean a shift from manual labor to administrative duties.

Many young men and women already active in a career in business, teaching, or industry have become interested in church-related vocations through active participation in the work of their churches. With faith in God and in response to his call they have left behind one career to make the necessary preparation for service in a church or denominational vocation. Their previous experience has often been a favorable asset to them—both in school and in their church-related vocations.

On the other hand, sometimes young people go into a church-related vocation under pressure or emotional impulse. One who does this should correct the mistake as soon as he discovers it.

4. *These Made the Change*

A successful young surgeon was an active church worker and an effective Christian witness in a North Carolina city. Feeling that his medical skill could be used in an area of more urgent need, he responded to God's direction and went with his wife and children to serve as a medical missionary. He changed not vocations but location.

A prosperous young businessman in Charlottesville, Virginia, was active in his church, in scouting, and other community affairs. Although active as a deacon, leader in Sunday school and Training Union in his church, he became convinced that he should give his whole time to a ministry of religious education. Selling his home, he moved his family to Louisville, Kentucky, for two years of intensive seminary training before going to serve a large church in Texas as minister of education. He changed both location and vocation.

Dr. C. C. Warren, former president of the Southern Baptist Convention and outstanding pastor, was a young lawyer when God called him to become a minister.

Ernest J. Loessner was working with the Florida State Highway Department when God called him into a religious education ministry. He resigned his position and enrolled as a student in the seminary, where he was later to become a professor of religious education.

No Christian should feel guilty about changing vocations if at each step he is earnestly seeking to know and to follow God's will.

5. *More Information Encourages New Decisions*

Thousands of Christian men and women now engaged in some other work declare that they once seriously considered entering a church-related vocation. For the lack of someone to counsel with them or of needed facts about the area of their interest, they passed up the call to a church-related vocation to enter some other field. Many such young people and young adults could regain a sense of satisfaction and serenity by "pulling up stakes" and preparing for the work they know God has called them to do.

Millions of Christians have chosen their vocations in business or industry with no real effort to find God's will for their lives and with no sense of serving God through their vocations. Every Christian should endeavor to listen to God's message to him about his vocational plans.

V. BEING CHRISTIAN IN EVERY VOCATION

A Christian can find God's will and serve him acceptably in a wide variety of vocations. God calls some Christians to serve him in business, in government, in public school teaching, in home and family life. He calls others to serve him in church-related vocations. It is the Christian's responsibility to find the place God has for him and to fill it to the best of his ability.

Some occupations are unworthy of a Christian. Worthy occupations can become channels of Christian service when they are entered by believers seeking to discover and to follow God's will. Before entering any vocation one should discover whether it offers opportunity for the fullest use of the talents, interests, and aptitudes which God has given him. A truly satisfactory vocation for a Christian will be work that meets human needs— physically, socially, intellectually, and spiritually. It will provide opportunities for bearing one's Christian witness to others and provide means for drawing people to a fellowship of Christian love.

1. *The Christian Way Is the Happiest Way*

Some misguided interpreters have supposed that the Bible teaches that God caused men to work as a punishment for sin. A more careful reading of the Scriptures will reveal that before sin entered the world God instructed Adam (Gen. 2 : 15) to cultivate and keep the garden of Eden. Undoubtedly a portion of the original happiness which characterized the garden of Eden was the opportunity which God gave to Adam to perform such useful work. There are few greater satisfactions in life than those found in a job well done.

To work with God, serving him faithfully, will make of life a thrilling adventure. The Christian knows that despite all difficulties he is able to do all things through Christ who strengthens him (Phil. 4 : 13). Life becomes not something to be dreaded and feared but a victory to be won.

The young Christian who has found God's will can say with Wordsworth:

> Bliss was it in that dawn to be alive,
> But to be young was very heaven!

2. *God's Way Is the Surest Way*

The poets have expressed this truth better than others. William Cullen Bryant, impressed by the unerring flight of migrating waterfowl, wrote concerning God's guidance:

> He who, from zone to zone,
>   Guides through the boundless sky thy certain flight,
> In the long way that I must tread alone
>   Will lead my steps aright.

The psalmist has expressed the serenity and security of God's followers in Psalm 23. The contrast between the security of the righteous and the ruin of the wicked is pictured in Psalm 1.

3. Christ's Way Is a Fruitful Way

How can a Christian live a fruitful life? Jesus gives the answer: "Abide in me, and I in you. As the branch cannot bear fruit of itself, except it abide in the vine; no more can ye, except ye abide in me. I am the vine, ye are the branches: He that abideth in me, and I in him, the same bringeth forth much fruit: for without me ye can do nothing" (John 15 : 4–5).

It is said that when William Booth, founder of the Salvation Army, was asked how he had been able to accomplish so much with so little, he replied, "If my life has been a success it is because God has had all there was of William Booth."

4. Christ's Way a Way of Sacrifice and Service

To live and work for Christ often demands real sacrifice. Dr. William Wallace was a beloved physician in a mission hospital in China when the communists gained control of the country. His witness for Christ and his love for the Chinese people, demonstrated in his deeds of mercy, made it difficult for the communists to persuade the Chinese that the Christian missionaries were not truly their friends. False charges were made against the faithful Christian doctor. He was imprisoned and later slain. He was "faithful unto death."

Jesus said to his disciples, "If any man will come after me, let him deny himself, and take up his cross daily, and follow me. For whosoever will save his life shall lose it; but whosoever will lose his life for my sake, the same shall save it" (Luke 9:23-24).

To the impetuous would-be follower who glibly promised, "Lord, I will follow thee whithersoever thou goest," Jesus responded, "Foxes have holes, and birds of the air have nests; but the Son of man hath not where to lay his head" (Luke 9:57-58).

Whatever the difficulties, Christian young people should seek to discover and accomplish God's will.

By serving God through his vocation, the Christian can help make this world into the kind of world that God wants it to be. Through dedicated vocations, every Christian can make his contribution to human happiness and welfare and find his own greatest self-fulfilment.

TOPICS FOR FURTHER DISCUSSION

1. If one should enter some work other than a church-related vocation, name ways in which such work could be done to glorify Christ.
2. Discuss the influence of parents in the vocational choices of their children.

CHAPTER 3 OUTLINE

I. TAKING A LOOK AT SELF

    1. What Talents Tell
    2. Interests and Disposition
    3. Measuring Physical Ability
    4. Overcoming Handicaps
    5. Emotional Stability
    6. A Pleasing Personality
    7. Intellectual Capacity
        (1) Ability differs
        (2) Intellectual ability can be cultivated
        (3) Methods of measurement
        (4) The test of performance

II. SECURING INFORMATION ABOUT VOCATIONS

    1. Through Counseling
    2. Printed Material and Films
    3. Church Vocations Counseling Committee
    4. Special Conferences
    5. Experience
    6. Seeking Help from Friends
    7. Use Available Help

III. TO EACH ACCORDING TO HIS ABILITY

    1. Opportunity Requires Responsibility
    2. Talents and Opportunities Differ
    3. A Task for All

3

God Equips All for Service

IF ONE is to follow the leadership of Christ in his career, he will need to discover what God has equipped him to do. Each person has aptitudes for a particular kind of work. One receives the greatest pleasure and satisfaction in exercising his strongest aptitudes. An individual who has a fine voice and musical skill will find his greatest joy in singing or playing a musical instrument. One who has artistic talent will love to paint, arrange flowers, or design clothes or a room. A person with oratorical gifts will enjoy public speaking. One who loves children and helping others learn will enjoy teaching.

It is reasonable to assume that if God has endowed a person with some particular talent God has a desire for him to use that talent in some way in his service. Knowing what he can do well should help a young person greatly in understanding what he should do about his vocation. It is therefore important that early in one's experience he should attempt to make a careful evaluation of his physical capacities, his emotional stability, his personality, his intellectual achievements, and other abilities with which he may be endowed.

To discover what God has equipped one to do, one should use all of the readily available methods of self-analysis. Intelligence and aptitude tests will indicate the areas of greatest strength and weakness and will reveal the areas in which one is most likely to succeed. School teachers, church leaders, businessmen, and personal friends can give wise counsel to those whom they know well about the areas in which they are likely to serve most effectively.

I. TAKING A LOOK AT SELF

What could possibly be more interesting for a young person than to take a look at himself? Most young people are tremendously interested in themselves and the vast possibilities of life. Taking a look at self is certainly important in the consideration of a vocation.

There are many factors in one's personality, one's interests, and one's abilities that deserve a careful and repeated look if he is to find God's will for his vocation.

1. *What Talents Tell*

Talents are as varied as individuals. What one enjoys doing most, and what one can do best may serve as clues in finding the right career.

Some people have many talents. Others have only limited talents. In either case the important thing is for each to follow the leadership of God into a vocation where he can render maximum service to God.

Some young people become anxious and disturbed because they do not have some obvious talent, such as musical or artistic ability.

One's talents usually fall into certain types which fit one for service in a group of related occupations which vocational counselors call "job families." An individual with a particular talent would probably do well in any of the vocations within a certain job family.

A young lady with an aptitude for artistic designing might do equally well as an interior decorator, a dress designer, or manager of an art gallery. A young man who enjoys working with people might be an effective executive, salesman, teacher, or social worker.

The United States Employment Service lists fifteen major job family groupings. Many different vocations may be related to any one of these job families. Each individual may wish to find the area in which his greatest abilities and interests lie. The job families are:

artists	public service	managerial
musical	technical	farming
literary	recording	cooking
entertainment	general clerical	child care
public contact	computing	personal service

Obviously, some jobs could be classified in several of the job families listed above. Such a list is valuable, however, in helping each individual to determine in what general area he is most interested and feels best equipped.

2. Interests and Disposition

One should study not only his talents but also his disposition if he is to discover God's vocation for his life. There are some people who are happiest and work best when they are dealing with things. They like to handle things, to make things, to invent things, to rearrange things. Others are happiest when dealing with people. They enjoy meeting people, being with people, and helping people. A third group are at their best when dealing with ideas.

Those who enjoy working with things rather than with

ideas will likely do well in some engineering or mechanical pursuit. Those who enjoy working with people will be more successful as teachers, preachers, social workers, nurses, athletic coaches, administrators, or salesmen. Those who enjoy working with ideas will likely find their greatest satisfaction as teachers, journalists, statisticians, public relations experts, or advertising managers.

Scientific studies reveal that one's vocational success and happiness are closely related to his general attitude toward life and to his opportunities for developing and growing as a person.

One's plans for a career, for education and preparatory experience should be vitally related to the physical, emotional, and mental equipment with which he has been endowed.

One should get all the facts possible in order to interpret God's purpose for his life. Inadequate information often results in misunderstanding God's will. Many capable young people have failed to get the educational preparation needed for work that really challenges their capacities. Proper encouragement might have led them into some of the hundreds of vocations now seeking trained people. Among these unfilled positions are thousands in the area of church-related vocations where positions remain unfilled for the lack of trained workers.

Much of the unhappiness discovered among people who feel that they are in the wrong vocation is due to a failure to relate God's call to their basic interests and aptitudes. Some people have lucrative jobs but are frustrated and unhappy because they feel that their work is neither a part of their real selves nor an expression of their deepest desires. Adequate vocational counseling would help to prevent such mistakes.

Unfortunately, some parents practically force their children into vocations against their will, only to see them fail miserably because they were never temperamentally suited for those jobs. The advice of father and mother can be helpful, but each individual should consider his own convictions and ideals and the counsel of informed Christian friends in seeking to find God's will.

Standardized tests such as the Kuder Preference Record, Form C,[1] or the Strong Vocational Interest Test,[2] may be of help in discovering the areas likely to be of greatest continuing interest and thus likely to be the most satisfying as a vocation. These tests may be administered by high school or college officials or by professional personnel or employment agencies.

The Kuder Preference Record Vocational Form C is a testing instrument designed to discover a person's real interests and thus enable him to prepare for the type of work that will bring maximum satisfaction.

The Strong Vocational Interest test reveals how an individual's interest patterns compare with those of people who are successful in a variety of occupations. It will be of help to the individual in clarifying his thinking about various vocations.

3. Measuring Physical Ability

Certain physical characteristics are important in many vocations. Yet many individuals have succeeded in such

[1] Published by Science Research Associates, 57 West Grand Avenue, Chicago 10, Illinois.

[2] Published by TESTSCOR, Minneapolis, Minnesota.

vocations despite physical handicaps. Through heroic efforts young people with serious speech defects have become effective public speakers. Others with crippled hands or club feet have become capable musicians. A weak and sickly lad named Theodore Roosevelt, through diligent effort, became a strong and stalwart leader of vast physical resources.

Although Napoleon was a small man, only five feet two inches tall, weighing one hundred and twenty pounds, he became the object of the affection and loyalty of thousands of soldiers. Many handicaps are more fancied than real. Most of them can be overcome through diligent and dedicated effort. Certainly each one can cultivate the habit of making the most of his native ability and appearance.

4. Overcoming Handicaps

Some emotional, mental, and physical conditions may make a person unsuitable for certain vocations. But he may be able to serve effectively in others. Serious physical disabilities, irreparable speech defects, or hereditary mental handicaps may indicate the need for special counseling to find work within the range of one's ability.

Many habits, traits, and attitudes which would make a person unfit for particular vocations may be overcome. Such characteristics as conceit, pride, laziness, carelessness, rudeness, and quarrelsomeness can be overcome by anyone desiring to make the necessary effort. Indeed, such habits should be put aside to achieve success in any vocation. Many young people do not realize how seriously they handicap their success in a career by carelessness in talk, appearance, or manners.

5. *Emotional Stability*

A leader in any field must be able to demonstrate stability of character and dependability in behavior. Childish, immature people are never able to challenge their followers to do effective work. Considerate, co-operative Christians reveal a daily personal reliance upon God.

Immature people may react with an attitude of "fight" or of "flight" when faced with problem situations. Either may become a serious personality problem. Many young people's groups have been disrupted by the childish behavior of someone old enough to know how to control his emotions.

Equally serious is the craze to "get away from it all," to escape from reality and responsibility through alcohol, other narcotics, or through frenzied efforts to find happiness and pleasure.

Several tests are available to help one check on his emotional stability, his personality and character traits. Professional counselors can explain to interested individuals the value of the Bernreuter, Minnesota Multiphasic, and Rohrschach tests, all of which can be helpful in determining one's emotional stability.

The Bernreuter Personality Inventory is a test designed to measure one's neurotic tendency, one's self-sufficiency, one's introversion-extroversion and dominance-submission tendencies.

One of the most widely used is the Rohrschach ink blot test. It is a projective personality test that must be administered by trained individuals. Under professional guidance the test will indicate how an individual goes about solving his problems, whether or not he is able to organize details into a meaningful whole.

The Rohrschach test and the similar Picture Preference Test can give valuable information to trained vocational counselors.

One's satisfaction and achievement in any career are greatly dependent upon his emotional stability. As good physical habits strengthen an individual for greater effectiveness physically, so one can develop good emotional habits that will enable him to work long hours under stress and strain without an emotional explosion or a physical collapse. Emotionally stable people will be able to control themselves, to adjust to changing circumstances and situations so as to make the largest possible contribution in the light of changing needs.

Criticism, conflict, and irritation can never destroy the serenity and spiritual power of the emotionally stable Christian. Nor will he ever feel any need to resort to such escapes or supposed emotional crutches as liquor or narcotics. He finds release from tension by diligent work, relaxing play, quiet meditation, and earnest prayer. The best solution for all emotional problems is this: "There is no fear in love; but perfect love casteth out fear" (1 John 4 : 18).

Emotional satisfaction is often more important than financial remuneration for the work one does. A young businessman in a southern city left a job paying $15,000 a year to become minister of education in his church. He and his wife found great satisfaction and joy in their new work. They have not spent their time lamenting the material luxury that they left in order to enter a church-related vocation. They found God's promise true as Paul expressed it, "My God shall supply all your need according to his riches in glory by Christ Jesus" (Phil. 4 : 19).

When one hears the statement, "I wouldn't do that job for a million dollars," he realizes that despite the almost universal emphasis in America today upon financial success, there are some things more important than financial returns, at least to some people.

What brings satisfaction in one's career? With some it may be a pleasant environment among congenial Christian friends. It may involve one's status in the community, the respect and admiration in which he is held by his peers.

Most Christians, however, will be satisfied when they are doing the work that they feel God has equipped them to do.

6. A Pleasing Personality

In analyzing one's qualifications and abilities for various vocations, one should examine his personality. Some vocations especially require a pleasing personality.

Far more people lose their jobs because of personality defects than for lack of ability.

Here is a place where a Christian can improve. Personality can be transformed. God has given to everyone the basic equipment and faculties for developing an acceptable personality. The kind of personality one develops is dependent upon his own choice. He can choose to be greedy and grasping, always looking out for his personal interests, or he can choose to be the devoted servant of others, seeking his greatest satisfaction in rendering loving service to those who need help. He can be kind and gracious in his personal relationships or he can be harsh and cruel. He can be quarrelsome or co-operative, a pusher or a persuader, a bully or a considerate friend. He can be "sloppy" in appearance, boisterous in conversation, vulgar in his thoughts, and vain in his conceits. But no one *has* to be like that. Everyone who sincerely wishes to do so can improve his personality.

Perhaps a personality inventory will help locate one's liabilities. Let each one study himself objectively and answer the following questions:

Do I like people?
Can I get along well with my friends and
family without quarrels?
Do I enjoy the company of both boys and
girls?
Do I avoid trying to excuse my failures
or blaming them on someone else?
Am I enthusiastic?
Am I courteous and well-poised?
Am I always willing to do my share?
Am I taking my place in church activities?
Am I relatively free from worry and inner
tensions?
Am I free from suspicion and jealousy?
Can I profit from my mistakes?
Can I overlook or laugh off unkind rebuffs
and snubs?
Am I cultivating daily devotions?

The more 'yes' answers you have, the higher your score. The 'no' answers reveal those areas in which some remedial work is required. [3]

One of the most important factors in the development of a pleasing Christian personality is the cultivation of

[3] Erma Paul Ferrari, *Careers for You* (Nashville: Abingdon, 1953), p. 36.

a genuine spirit of love for others. When one really loves other people, he becomes concerned for their welfare as much as for his own needs. The disagreeable person who is egotistical, self-centered, vain, bitter, and cynical has never learned the art of loving as Christ teaches one to love.

7. Intellectual Capacity

(1) *Ability differs.*—People do not have the same intellectual ability. Although all known methods of measuring intelligence are relative and fallible it is possible to discover a wide difference between individuals. Adequate motivation and interest make it possible to rise above certain intellectual limitations. However, one avoids frustration and failure if he is willing to follow God's leadership for his vocation within the reasonable limits indicated by his mental ability. All vocations require intelligence but there are many successful people who have compensated for intellectual limitations and lack of formal training.

(2) *Intellectual ability can be cultivated.*—Schools are committed to the training of the intellect. The buildings, equipment, teachers, and materials provided are there to stimulate and direct the developing intellectual pursuits of the students. Unfortunately, many young people fail to take advantage of these opportunities and therefore limit the type and the quality of service that they are able to render throughout their lives.

By the time one has reached the Young People's department he should have left behind the laziness and carelessness that often mark the immature adolescent. With the completion of high school and college it be-

comes obvious that one's study habits and faithfulness
to a task are important factors in vocational placement.

The important jobs in business, industry, science, and
the professions go to those willing to study diligently
and persistently. Those filling these key administrative
posts are people who did not put their books away on
graduation day but continued to study the latest develop-
ments in their own fields and who kept up with what was
going on in their vocations.

(3) *Methods of measurement.*—There are many methods of taking one's mental measure. The observation of
parents and friends is such a measurement. It may begin
with the proud boasts of an enthusiastic mother or grand-
mother and so continue on through life. A more objective
and widely used method of measuring intelligence is the
intelligence test. Even though intelligence tests are reli-
able and helpful, they are not perfect. They indicate
only that in the particular facet of life being measured
through that test one has or does not have certain abilities.

One may be able to succeed very well in certain vocations despite a weakness at the point tested. Yet such
tests do help to eliminate from one's career plans those
vocations requiring abilities he obviously does not possess.

There are many forms of intelligence tests—some
verbal, some nonverbal; some for use with individuals,
some for use with groups. Generally the individual tests
such as the Stanford-Binet and Wechsler-Bellevue are
more accurate than the group tests, though the latter are
usually used in large schools.

Remember, most psychological tests are designed to be administered by well-trained specialists. Their chief value is to predict success or failure in a given area. They are limited in their ability to give definite conclusions upon which to determine God's will for one's vocation. They do give information that can guide in counseling and indicating the direction in which God seems to be leading.

(4) *The test of performance.*—One of the best means of determining one's intellectual ability is the widely used test of performance. Successful performance is a commonly accepted indication of ability. An individual may discover some indication of the type of work in which God wants him by looking objectively at his past performance.

Some measurements of performance are to be found in school grades, in the positions occupied in school clubs, in the success achieved in some particular job, and in the positions of service one fills in his church and community.

II. Securing Information About Vocations

In determining one's fitness for a particular vocation, it is important to secure as much accurate information about that vocation as possible. In addition to the study of this book and related books suggested, opportunities may be provided in various church groups.

1. *Through Counseling*

Intelligent understanding of God's purpose for one's life will require the greatest possible information. Many schools, churches, and other community agencies are now making it possible for young people to become more thoroughly acquainted with the various vocations. Career conferences in high school and college, in which representatives of various vocations discuss the preparation for work of the various fields, help young people to know more about what is involved in various vocations.

2. *Printed Material and Films*

Much literature is now being prepared and made available to help young people in following God's will for their vocations. Books, pamphlets, charts, tracts, pictures, and many kinds of tests are available.

This book is one of a series published by the Sunday School Board dealing with vocations. The Sunday School Board has a staff busy in the preparation of vocational guidance materials, in directing conferences, and assisting with vocational clinics.

The Southern Baptist Foreign Mission Board, Box 5148, Richmond 20, Virginia, has available several pamphlets that will be of help to those interested in vocations in foreign mission service. These include "Get Ready for a Real Job," a sixteen page booklet designed to help a person evaluate his call and qualifications for service as a foreign missionary. "The How of Missionary Appointment" is an eight page tract explaining the procedure of missionary appointment by the Foreign Mission Board. It indicates the basic educational requirements along with the qualifications needed for service in foreign missions.

"You, a Missionary," is an eight page tract explaining the opportunities of service as a missionary. Necessary qualifications, including educational preparation, practical experience, physical health, emotional stability, and consecration to Christ, are discussed. The tract answers such questions as how to get started, how to be appointed, who will help, and what is ahead for the missionary.

Another helpful booklet is "Needed Overseas." It shows the opportunity for mission service in the areas of church development, Christian education, and medical service.

Of special interest for those planning a nursing career is another pamphlet from the Foreign Mission Board, entitled "More Nurses Are Needed Now."

All who are interested in foreign mission service should contact the personnel department of the Foreign Mission Board, Box 5148, Richmond 20, Virginia.

From the Southern Baptist Home Mission Board, 161 Spring Street, North West, Atlanta 3, Georgia, one may secure the tract "Whom Shall I Send?" which outlines the qualifications for home missionaries. It describes the various fields of service, how salaries are determined, and other provisions made for those in home mission service.

Also available from the Home Mission Board are tracts describing the student summer mission program and the Southern Baptist Tentmaker program. The first of these describes a program through which several hundred college and seminary students serve during the summer on some of the mission fields.

The Southern Baptist Tentmaker program describes the opportunity for those willing to take secular jobs in pioneer mission areas and in addition serve to establish or strengthen Southern Baptist mission work there.

From the Education Commission of the Southern Baptist Convention, 127 Ninth Avenue, North, Nashville 3, Tennessee, may be secured the magazine *Career News*. The subscription price is $1.00 per year. It brings up-to-date information about various vocational areas. The Education Commission also publishes a series of tracts on careers in various vocations and other helpful pamphlets such as "Finding a Worthy Career," "Christ and My Future," and "Planning for College" (single copies ten cents each).

Information may be secured from each of the Southern Baptist seminaries describing the courses available. In addition, some also publish tracts that are helpful to those who are considering church-related vocations.

In the Bibliography will be found a list of other valuable books and pamphlets available.

Excellent books and other materials related to vocational counseling are now available in many high school and college libraries and counseling offices.

Films on vocational guidance are listed in the catalogue *Focus*, which may be obtained and the films rented from your Baptist Book Store.

3. *Church Vocations Counseling Committee*

Increasingly the churches are accepting greater responsibility for aiding those seeking vocational guidance. There may be in many churches people peculiarly well-qualified to serve on a vocational counseling committee. The following responsibilities are suggested for such a committee:

Work with the pastor and the other church leaders in setting up a church program of vocational counseling for all of the young people in the church.

Work out plans for a year-round program of vocational counseling.

See that the philosophy of Christian vocations is presented regularly through the various church organizations and worship services.

Supply available literature on vocational counseling and the necessary preparation to all interested young people of the church.

Be aware of the needs in church-related vocations and keep these before the young people of the church.

Counsel with young people interested in various vocations concerning the necessary educational preparation.

Plan career conferences and other counseling services during Youth Week or on other special occasions.

Secure information about vocational counseling available in summer assemblies, conventions, and other such occasions outside the church.

Encourage young people to make direct contact with various agencies in the denomination equipped to give them further assistance.

4. *Special Conferences*

Some churches will desire to conduct career conferences, enlisting the assistance of professionally trained people to give aptitude tests and other helpful information. Representatives from various professions may tell about vocational opportunities in their professions. Each speaker should give a description of his vocation, including the nature of the work, hours, working conditions, attractive and undesirable features about the work, and its future possibilities. He should also present the educational requirements of the vocation, the personal qualifications that would make for success in the vocation, and the physical qualifications involved.

Each speaker or conference leader representing a particular vocation should point out the satisfactions and the rewards that come through that vocation. Such questions as how to start in the vocation and where one can find further information about it should be answered.

Such vocational guidance may be made available in the summer assemblies conducted by church and denominational agencies.

5. *Experience*

Each summer the mission boards and the Student Department of the Baptist Sunday School Board promote a summer mission program. This program enables many young people to discover firsthand the needs and the opportunities in several church-related vocations.

Summertime and after-school jobs in stores, shops, and offices enable many young people to experiment with various vocations.

In many schools there is a distributive education program which enables young people to attend school part of the day and to spend another period each day in actual experience in some vocation in which they are interested.

Various branches of the armed forces provide vocational training for young people in military service.

6. *Seeking Help from Friends*

It is sometimes difficult for a young person to separate his wishes from his abilities. His ambitions are likely to color his thinking about his ability. A real friend and wise counselor can give unselfish and unbiased advice concerning the relation of one's abilities to God's plan for his vocation. Such counsel may offer suggestions about courses of action that have not been considered by the individual.

7. *Use Available Help*

However, many young people with these opportunities for discovering more about the various vocations fail to take advantage of their opportunities and drift into vocations in which they are not happy and which bring them no sense of satisfaction and achievement. If one is to get the help needed in finding God's will, he must utilize the facilities that are available. One must take advantage of the literature, the counsel, and available experience that will lead him to an intelligent understanding of the vocation to which God would call him.

III. To Each According to His Ability

1. *Opportunity Requires Responsibility*

In Matthew 25 : 14–30 is found the record of a rich businessman who called his servants and delivered unto them his goods.

Different amounts were given to each of the servants, "to each according to his several ability" (Matt. 25:15).

There was the expectation that each servant would use the goods entrusted to him wisely and fruitfully.

The obvious purpose of this story was to emphasize that God expects each of his followers to use wisely the talents which he has been given. The quality and the quantity of talents may differ, but each one is expected to do his best with whatever talents he may possess.

Every Christian will want to take a personal inventory to discover the talents which God has given him. Has God given the ability to sing? Then that talent must be used for him. Has God given artistic skill? Then it must be used to present the story of Christian love, to express one's devotion and worship of Almighty God, and to bring joy to one's fellow men. Has God given administrative ability and business judgment? These, too, should be dedicated to his service and be used for him, whether in a church-related vocation or in the many other occupations where Christians can serve.

2. Talents and Opportunities Differ

No two individuals have the same talents. There are many different abilities as well as many different opportunities of service. Paul points this out in his letter to the Corinthians, "There are diversities of gifts, but the same Spirit" (1 Cor. 12 : 4).

Paul then goes on to mention many of the differing gifts that are given to Christians and concludes, "All these worketh that one and the selfsame Spirit, dividing to every man severally as he will. For as the body is one, and hath many members, and all the members of that one body, being many, are one body: so also is Christ" (1 Cor. 12 : 11–12).

In Ephesians 4 : 11 Paul lists those whom God gave to the church as special gifts for their benefit: "And he gave some, apostles; and some, prophets; and some, evangelists; and some, pastors and teachers." All of these, Paul adds, were given to the church in order that they might prepare all of the church members for Christian service to build up the body of Christ which is the church.

3. A Task for All

God has a task for every person. The Christian will seek to discover that particular task for which he has been divinely equipped. Having found that area of service where it seems that God has called him to serve most effectively, the Christian will prepare to use his divinely given talents to the best advantage through diligent preparation and faithful service.

In the work of the world every Christian can be used, whether as a farmer, a laborer, a mechanic, as a business or professional man; whether as a homemaker, a nurse, or a schoolteacher; whether occupied in some church-related vocation or in some lay vocation. Each is under obligation to use the talents which God has given him so as to make his contribution to human welfare.

PROJECTS FOR CLASS PARTICIPATION

1. Plan a vocational guidance program for the church, using parents, church and community leaders to meet the needs of young people in the church and community.
2. Plan a Career Night for a youth fellowship, or a week-end Career Conference. Secure information about Vocational Emphasis Week sponsored by the Baptist Student Union.
3. Plan a conference period for parents to discuss how to counsel with their children about vocations.
4. Check on available locations for taking aptitude tests and other specialized guidance in selecting a vocation.

CHAPTER 4 OUTLINE

I. YOUTH TIME IS DECISION TIME

II. LOOK ON THE FIELDS
1. Fitting Talents to Service
2. Hearing God's Call
3. All of Life Sacred
4. God Has Many Places of Service
5. A Suggested Formula

III. EXAMINING POSSIBLE VOCATIONS
1. Serving in the Church
2. Local Church Ministries
3. Denominational Positions
    (1) Foreign missions
    (2) Home missions
    (3) Sunday School Board
    (4) State mission boards
    (5) Woman's Missionary Union
    (6) Baptist Student Union director
    (7) Other denominational agencies
4. Building a Christian Home
5. Business
6. The Professions

IV. CHANGING VOCATIONAL INTERESTS
1. Changes Coming with Maturity
2. Changes Growing Out of Christian Dedication

V. WHAT NEXT?
1. Record the Decision Publicly
2. Associate with Like-minded Friends
3. Respond Willingly

4

Answering God's Call

"PASTOR, could you help me? I'll soon be graduating, and I need to decide soon what I should do with my life." The pastor gladly arranged a conference with the apprehensive high school senior.

A college freshman sought out his Baptist student director. "You know, John," he said, "I've been doing a lot of heavy thinking lately. When I left home last fall I was a crazy mixed-up kid. But more and more I've been thinking that I'm about to see things straighten out. I think God has a place for me, some particular place. I need somebody to help me find out just what it is."

Another college student was back home from a student missions conference, bubbling over with enthusiasm. "I've found it," she exclaimed to her parents. "I've found what it is that God wants me to do. As I heard that missionary tell about the need for Christian teachers in Africa, I knew God wanted me to use my life serving him there."

I. YOUTH TIME IS DECISION TIME

1. *Vocational Decision Time*

Youth time is decision time. Many high school seniors feel the pressure of having to make some kind of a decision for which they are not prepared. College students faced with the choice of majors are concerned with making the right decisions. Many young people feel the Holy Spirit leading them to some field of dedicated Christian Service. When God speaks, his followers should be eager to respond.

2. Help from Leaders

Pastors, youth workers, Sunday school teachers, and other sensitive and helpful Christian leaders are approached often by eager young people seeking to know God's plan for their lives. Earnestly these young people survey the various fields of service to find the places where their divinely given talents can render the greatest service to mankind.

Finding one's lifework may not be easy. It may require the assistance of counselors at school or at church, of pastor, friends, and family. If one is to succeed in any career he must plan wisely and obtain needed counsel from others equipped to assist. Specialized help which all may need in following God's will is available in schools and colleges, in churches, community centers, and denominational offices. A long series of interviews, tests, and experiments may be required to find the place of service one is best equipped to fill.

A person will not get all the help needed in making a vocational choice by one conversation with his pastor, by taking a few tests, or by reading a few books (including this one!). Finding the place God has for one's life is a continuous process with the necessity for constant contact with God in prayer and continuing obedient service. As one step is taken by faith and in obedience to God's direction, he then reveals what he would have one do next. God directs sometimes by opening doors, at other times by closing doors.

II. LOOK ON THE FIELDS

1. *Fitting Talents to Service*

In seeking to follow Christ in one's career, it is important not only that the individual take a look at himself but also that he examine carefully the fields of service. After a person has discovered his talents, he can then more intelligently understand where they can best be invested for maximum Christian service.

In this search, every worthy vocation that would utilize one's divinely given talents should be carefully and prayerfully studied with a view to discovering that ministry which God has planned for one's life.

Whether one's life is to be given to agriculture, medicine, nursing, salesmanship, construction, or to some church-related ministry, a young Christian is under obligation to find God's will for himself and to serve in the vocation in which he can feel that he is fulfilling God's plan for his life.

2. *Hearing God's Call*

To assert that all are called to make their vocations Christian does not minimize the supernatural element in a call to life service but rather widens the scope of such a call to insist that every Christian must seek to find God's particular place for his life.

3. All of Life Sacred

The Christian cannot properly divide vocations into the secular and the sacred. All of life should be sacred and every individual should perform his vocational service as unto God. No Christian should enter or continue in any vocation that is contrary to God's will.

4. God Has Many Places of Service

Some young people have the mistaken idea that in order to serve the Lord, one must get on the pay roll of a church or denominational agency. Now, certainly, God needs staff members on the mission field and in the churches of the homeland. But God also needs Christian businessmen, Christian housewives, Christian school-teachers, Christian doctors, Christian nurses, and many, many others who will serve Christ in their vocations and as leaders in their churches as loyally and faithfully as the men and women called of God to serve as members of church staffs or as employees of denominational agencies.

5. A Suggested Formula

Some years ago, Dr. William Russell Owen gave three rules for finding God's will for one's life: follow the gleam, favor your bent, and enter the open door.

III. EXAMINING POSSIBLE VOCATIONS

As the Christian young person surveys the various fields of service, he will want to be aware of the relative needs in each of these vocations. The Christian will want to invest his life where his vocational service will render some benefit to mankind.

For the Christian, any vocation to which God may call will be one of full-time Christian service. Some will serve in church-related vocations as paid workers in a church, institution, or denominational organization. Others will earn their living in some other way and give their available time as volunteers in Christian service.

1. Serving in the Church

Because of the great need for well-trained and dedicated leaders in the churches at home and on the mission field, Christian young people ought to consider the various areas of Christian service within the church and the denomination.

(1) *The demands are high.*—Working on a church staff is Christian service of a high order. Such work demands people with superior ability and sincere Christian faith.

What work is more enduring or significant than that performed by the churches and their agencies? Where can one take hold of the world's need more directly and lift mankind more effectively than through the ministry of the church? Here in the varied phases of its ministry of love may be found opportunities of service to challenge the finest, most capable young people.

Writers, editors, preachers, teachers, doctors, nurses, administrators, secretaries—all, and more, are needed now in church-related positions. Every young Christian may properly ask: Has God given me the abilities, interests, and skills that should be invested in the work of his church? Could it be that God is calling me into service through the church? If God should call, would I be willing to respond?

(2) *Is this God's plan?*—A response to God's call to enter a church-related vocation is usually the outgrowth of an earlier commitment of one's life to the Lordship of Christ.

It is proper that every Christian should give consideration to this area of church-related service, giving to his Lord and to his church prior claims upon the investment of his life. Dr. I. J. Van Ness, who became executive secretary of the Baptist Sunday School Board, was started on his career of Christian service by the arresting question of his pastor, Dr. J. P. Dickenson. He asked young Van Ness what good reason he might have for not giving his life to the Christian ministry.

That is a question that every young Christian should be prepared to answer. Does one have talents that could be used in some church-related vocation? Does one have an inclination to render such service? Is there a willingness to offer one's life and talents to be used in such a ministry? Has God clearly indicated that he has some other life plan?

2. *Local Church Ministries*

There are three basic divisions of church ministries within the church-related vocational field. These are the pastoral ministry, the ministry of music, and the ministry of religious education.

(1) *Pastor.*—Most young people are familiar with what is involved in the pastoral ministry. They know that a pastor directs the program of a church, prepares ser-

mons, counsels with the lost, the bereaved, and the troubled, marries the young and sometimes the not so young, and buries the dead.

The pastor's task is not easy, yet he does his work gladly and without complaint because he finds joy in doing what God has called him to do.

Claude U. Broach has some helpful counsel for those considering the pastoral ministry. "You ought to know what the preacher's job really is. The common idea includes four activities: preach on Sunday (one good sermon and one not so good), read, play golf, and draw a salary. Add to this a little visiting, conduct weddings and funerals, and there you have the popular picture of the ministry.

"But, take it from me—or from any other preacher— that's not the ministry! The ministry is a slave driving job if you've got a conscience. For example, you don't get sermons out of thin air—not real sermons which show depth of thought, awareness of human needs, speaking the language of today with the overtones of eternity. You have to do real digging for sermons that change the patterns of human thought and reveal Christ the great Disturber who ever makes men discontent with themselves as they are.

"Visiting is no easy job either. And you must do it gladly—the sick, the sorrowing, the disgruntled, the lost, the wicked, the rich, the poor—all of them.

"Your life as a preacher is public property. Some of those who help to pay your salary will think that gives them the right to prescribe your conduct and will expect you to be accountable to them rather than to your Lord.

"Have you ever heard of the loneliness of leadership? It will get you in the ministry. Your friendships will be limited because you can't show any favoritism.

"And your salary! If you go on to get a doctor's degree, it will mean that you will spend as much time in preparation as the physician, more than the lawyer, more than the average college professor. But your salary scale will not stack up with theirs. Do you mind?

"So you want to be a preacher! There are three things you should face before you decide. First, and most important, has God called you into the ministry? It is not a profession. It is a calling. Has God called you? Unless you can be deathlessly sure, you'd better do something else.

"Second, do you genuinely love folks? Just plain folks, with all their idiosyncrasies, their prejudices, their sins, their littleness, their goodness, their greatness? Can you be patient with them all in spite of everything? If you carry a chip on your shoulder, your feelings on your sleeve, for mercy's sake get in a job where you can pout without making the kingdom of God suffer for your littleness!

"Finally, are you willing to work? If the ministry seems an easy job, it's your fault. But if you want to bring in the kingdom of God, if you want the religion of Jesus let loose to revolutionize human lives, you'll have to work! Headwork, heartwork, and footwork!"

(2) *Minister of music.*—Music and religion have always been closely associated. Every program of the church must have a capable leader, and music is no exception. Each church should enlist the finest and best-trained leadership for its music.

Churches today are becoming acutely aware of the ever-increasing need for some qualified person to head and direct the total music ministry of the church. More and more churches are delegating this responsibility to a full-time minister of music. From every section of the country there comes the call for those who are capable, consecrated, and prepared for this field of Christian service.

Churches with small memberships and limited budgets frequently have a combination minister of music and education or a combination of music and some other area of work. Such a worker must have training in both areas. There are some churches that have a combination organist-director. In such a position a person must have training in two fields of music—choral and organ.

With this increasing demand for the full-time minister of music or combination worker comes the need for clarifying and defining his responsibilities.

a. Duties of the minister of music.—The over-all task of the minister of music is that of organizing and maintaining a churchwide music ministry. The minister of music has direct responsibility for all music in the church, including the various services, organizations, agencies, and activities. He should make available to the entire church membership a systematic and continuous plan of music training, instruction, and participation.

He should seek to develop a fully graded, comprehensive, church music ministry which will enlist people, train their talents, magnify worship, promote evangelism, and benefit all ages and organizations. His responsibilities encompass much more than choir directing and song leading. He is minister of music to the entire church, and the church should look to him as such.

b. The church music ministry.—A comprehensive, church-wide music ministry functions in five specific areas: (1) congregational activities, which include the development of congregational singing, regular hymn rehearsals, annual carol sings, and the promotion of good music in all church organizations through trained leadership; (2) choral activities, which include all the graded choirs and vocal ensembles; (3) instrumental activities, which include the development of competent organists and pianists, a church orchestra, and the training of instrumental ensembles and soloists; (4) training activities, which include the development of abilities and proficiency in all the musicians, and the training of leadership and membership; and (5) promotional activities, which utilize the many promotional means for the development of a comprehensive music education program.

(3) *Minister of education.*—Less familiar to many young people are the many phases of the nonpastoral ministry. To respond to a call to the church educational ministry is to follow in the footsteps of Jesus the teacher. His ministry was a teaching as well as a preaching and healing ministry (Matt. 4:23). The early church was a teaching church (Acts 5:42). If our churches today are to follow the New Testament pattern, they too must give a large emphasis to a continuing educational ministry. The minister of education is the leader of the educational program of the church. His duties are discussed briefly.

a. A teacher and interpreter of God's Word.—To be an effective "teacher of teachers" the minister of education will be an interpreter of the Christian message. As the pastor interprets the Bible in the pulpit, the minister of education in the teacher's meetings, training courses, church paper, and through other available media seeks to prepare as effective interpreters Sunday school teachers, Training Union leaders, and others whom he is able to enlist and train for service in the church and community. His organizational and promotional skills will be designed to reach more people with the Christian message and to instruct them in the Christian way of life.

b. An educational administrator.—Just as public schools need principals, supervisors, and superintendents, so the educational organizations of the churches need administrators.

The minister, or director, of education plans with the other church leaders for the enlargement and more effective functioning of the church's educational ministry. He will lead the church to survey the needs and possibilities of the community it serves; to project an organization of well-trained leaders able to enlist, teach, and win; and to develop all of the available prospects in the community.

The minister of education will enlist prospective workers in a continuous program of leadership training designed to develop skills and understanding for the beginning worker and to improve the effectiveness of the workers already serving.

The minister of education will lead the church to make adequate provision for effective Christian teaching in suitable buildings, properly equipped with curriculum materials and teaching aids needed for effective teaching and learning.

All of these responsibilities mean that the minister of

education will spend his time in personal conferences with workers and prospective workers, in serious study of the Bible and of more effective ways of using its truths in meeting human needs, and in attending conventions, conferences, and assemblies where he can share ideas with other Christian leaders. He will answer the questions and deal with the problems arising in such a comprehensive educational program as is now found in many churches.

(4) *Other educational workers.*—Many churches today require other educational workers. Some of these workers are listed here.

a. Educational specialists.—Age group workers are used in many of the larger churches to give specialized guidance to a particular age group. For example, a director of children's activities may be employed to give supervision to the work of all church organizations ministering to children from birth through eight years of age. The same church may have a Junior worker giving her time to the Juniors and their leaders in Sunday school, Training Union, missionary organizations, and recreation. Many churches now employ youth directors. Such workers require seminary training with specialized instruction in the needs of the age groups.

b. Church secretarial work.—Dedicated young women with proper business training are able to make a vital contribution to the work of their churches as church secretaries. They are responsible for typing and filing the correspondence of the pastor and the church staff, for keeping the church membership rolls accurate, and for preparing church bulletins, announcements, and mimeographed material used in the church program.

They may handle the financial records of the church and order the literature and supplies.

Educational secretaries give a part of their time to the promotion and direction of the church educational program in addition to their secretarial duties.

c. Church hostess.—Many churches are employing a church hostess who is responsible for preparing the meals served at the church and for assisting the various groups which plan for refreshments in connection with their activities.

d. Recreation director.—Some churches are employing trained recreation leaders to direct a graded program of recreation for the various age groups in the church.

3. *Denominational Positions*

The Baptist World Alliance, the Southern Baptist Convention Executive Committee, the various state conventions, and the local (district) associations offer many opportunities for vocational service utilizing a wide variety of talents.

The Baptist World Alliance, the Executive Committee, and the various boards and agencies of the Southern Baptist Convention employ administrators usually known as executive secretaries. Each of these boards and agencies has a staff. Some of them employ many people.

(1) *Foreign missions.*—Serving under the Foreign Mission Board are pastors, evangelists, teachers, educational workers, and musicians who do on the foreign mission field much the same type of work that these individuals do in the churches in the homeland. Included on the Foreign Mission Board staff are many doctors and nurses who operate hospitals and minister to the sick

on the mission fields. Other missionaries teach in the mission schools, such as kindergartens, grade schools, high schools, colleges, and seminaries operated in the various fields. Also needed are secretaries, office managers, bookkeepers, and other administrative officers.

(2) *Home missions.*—The Home Mission Board employs workers to perform similar functions for service here in the homeland. Educational, evangelistic, and social workers serve many racial minorities and underprivileged groups in the United States. Work in Cuba, Alaska, and the Canal Zone is under the direction of the Home Mission Board.

(3) *Sunday School Board.*—The Baptist Sunday School Board performs many functions. It employs people to write, edit, print, distribute, and promote the use of denominational literature, books, films, and other aids to effective Christian education. Included in the Board's ministry are church architects, statisticians, church librarians, recreation directors, producers and distributors of visual aids, artists, advertising directors, accountants, salesmen, and personnel directors. All of these are needed to supply the churches with the materials and equipment so essential for maximum effectiveness.

(4) *State mission boards.*—Hundreds of persons are employed by the state Baptist conventions in administrative, educational, and promotional activities concerned with the work of Sunday school, Training Union, church music, Brotherhood, Baptist Student Union, stewardship, evangelism, public relations, and the organization of new churches and missions. Each Baptist state organization has its own Baptist paper, with an editor and staff. Each has its children's home with a staff

of workers. In many states, the associational missionaries work under the supervision of the state mission program.

(5) *Woman's Missionary Union.*—Both the Convention-wide and state organizations of Woman's Missionary Union employ persons in administrative, educational, and office activities in the promotion of the missionary objectives of this fine auxiliary.

(6) *Baptist Student Union director.*—The position of the Baptist Student Union director is uniquely related to the college campus, but unquestionably is a church-related vocation. The director of the Baptist Student Union is responsible for the spiritual welfare of the Baptist students enrolled in the school he serves. His primary purpose is to lead the Baptist students in a program of Christian growth through church enlistment, campus evangelism, and Christian studentship. He is the direct link between the denomination and the thousands of Baptists who enrol in tax-supported and private schools. He is the co-ordinator of student religious activities on the Baptist campuses.

In the main, there are three requirements of a Baptist Student Union director.

a. B.S.U. member.—The Baptist Student Union director should have experience as a volunteer worker in the educational program of a church and as a member of the B.S.U. during his college days. The life of the Baptist Student Union has, is, and shall be a realistic linking of the student with a local church program during college days. The student who is loyal to his church in college finds it much easier to adjust to a normal way of life after graduation.

b. Advanced college training.—The Baptist Student

Union director should have academic training which would make him feel at home in the climate of the university or college campus where he works, enabling him to teach God's Word, preparing him for his role as counselor, and equipping him for leadership. This role of promoter, teacher, and counselor demands a minimum of a Bachelor's degree from an accredited college and a Master's degree or a Bachelor of Divinity degree. His graduate training ideally should include study in the graduate fields of Bible, religious education, theology, psychology, counseling, and philosophy.

c. Missionary in a strategic field.—Charles Roselle, state student secretary of Tennessee, sums it up in the following statement: "Truly the Baptist student director is a chosen missionary for he ministers to one of the most strategic mission fields in all the world—the modern university campus. He plays many roles—counselor to the football player, adviser in the fraternity house, member on the student activities' committee. In each varied activity, however, the director's purpose is the same: to represent Christ on the campus where blow the winds of many philosophies.

"'The spiritual coach' best describes the Baptist student director. He does not play the game for the student, but encourages and advises the students who compose Christ's team on that campus. He coaches at a critical time in the lives of the players—when they are making life-lasting and eternity-shaping decisions concerning marriage, vocation, and religious commitment. Many teams will demand the attention of each player during the game so the spiritual coach must be properly prepared to present the claims of Christ."

(7) *Other denominational agencies.*—Other Baptist agencies give opportunity for Christian service to those with highly specialized skills as in the fields of radio and television, insurance, hospital administration, and educational administration.

The need for more workers in church-related positions is urgent.

4. *Building a Christian Home*

Another Christian vocation that ought to be continually magnified is that of homemaker. Homemaking is a vocation established by God in the garden of Eden, and has through the centuries been a major area of service to God.

Marriage is a part of God's plan. Each young woman should enter into marriage with a sense of divine direction and should seek to make her home Christian by obedience to God in every family relationship.

Work, including housework, is not a curse because of man's sin. God gave to Adam and Eve the responsibility of caring for the garden before sin entered the world. God is a worker. Jesus said, "My Father worketh hitherto, and I work" (John 5:17). Surely the self-sacrificing labor of a godly wife and mother can be used as a means of honoring Christ who has called her into the Christian service of homemaking. God blesses and sustains the Christian mother who is busy caring for her children and her husband, keeping her home clean and happy.

A particularly blessed privilege and opportunity is to serve God as the wife of one who serves in some church-related vocation. To respond to God's call to such a life is to share in the special joys of those who give all their strength and energy to unselfish service for others. Such a life is not always easy. Wives of ministers, like those of doctors and others in similar service to mankind, must be willing to share their husbands with a busy career. They must understand the demands people often make upon their husbands. They must give encouragement when needed and gently and tactfully puncture the inflated ego of husbands who succumb to flattery.

To the vocation of homemaking more women will give themselves than to any other, and in this sphere of service they will find their greatest opportunities, as wives and mothers, in the building of Christian homes.

5. Business

Under this heading should be included a wide variety of activities such as agriculture, construction, manufacturing, transportation, advertising, sales, communication, and related vocations so important to the well-ordered functioning of modern society. In each there are opportunities for fruitful Christian service.

6. The Professions

In addition to those professions included under church-related vocations the dedicated Christian may feel God's call to serve in the professions of medicine, law, politics, education, or the arts. In each of these areas specialization offers wide opportunities of service.

IV. CHANGING VOCATIONAL INTERESTS

1. Changes Coming with Maturity

The first vocational interests among small children are

usually in the direction of such active, exciting occupations as fireman, policeman, detective, or cowboy. As children grow older their interests turn to those vocations having greater prestige, such as doctors, statesmen, lawyers, and business executives.

As they develop further, many young people are able to look more objectively at their abilities and choose a vocation which sometimes represents a compromise between what they would like to be and what they think they can become. However, mature Christian young people will understand that God has a purpose for every life and will follow his leadership in finding their places of vocational service.

These experiences are tremendously affected by the social groups of which one may be a part such as one's family, school group, and church organizations. Other social pressures are exerted through the press, radio, television, and the movies.

2. Changes Growing Out of Christian Dedication

No one should be embarrassed to change from an earlier vocational commitment which, after further study of his abilities, seems not to be the proper place of service. The Christian will wisely keep the door of his mind and heart open for continuing spiritual guidance in the matter of vocational service.

Only when Christian young people have analyzed their lives to discover what God has equipped them to do, and when they have taken a careful look at the various fields of service, will they be able to interpret God's call intelligently as to the particular places of service in which God may want them to serve.

The Christian will want to serve in that place where he will find the maximum opportunity to express himself in releasing the potentialities built up within human beings. The Christian will want to invest his life in some creative lifework where he can get under the load of human need and lift it.

V. WHAT NEXT?

After one has given diligent and prayerful study to the various possibilities for a life career in the will of God, he will come ultimately to a settled conviction about the matter. After one has found God's will for his life, what should he do next?

1. *Record the Decision Publicly*

When one has responded to God's call it is always helpful for that decision to be shared with others. There are many who will be able to help him in making adequate plans for the realization of his vocational purpose, whatever the vocational calling may be. For those still in high school and college, teachers and school administrators can assist in planning the educational preparation needed for maximum effectiveness in the particular vocation. Leaders in the church and denomination can be of great help if their counsel is sought.

Any who feel led to enter some church-related vocation should write to the church-related vocations counselor, Baptist Sunday School Board, 127 Ninth Avenue, North, Nashville 3, Tennessee, indicating his name, age, address, educational status at present, and the vocation to which he feels God is calling. Letters to the colleges and seminaries which one may be interested in attending

will bring further information about entrance requirements and other factors to be considered in securing educational preparation.

2. *Associate with Like-minded Friends*

In many schools there are clubs organized around various vocational interests. Activities in a science club, a
music club, and other groups with special interests may
be the source of much helpful information.

Many churches will have informal groups within the
church composed of all of those who have committed
themselves to some church-related vocation. In such
groups they must learn about the types of service to be
performed in various vocations in the church and denomination and the preparation required. Such groups may
provide opportunities for service, giving practical experience in some church-related ministry.

3. *Respond Willingly*

There is no virtue in delaying one's response to God's
call. Whenever God makes his way clear, the Christian
should respond promptly and gladly, knowing that his
highest joy will come in doing the will of God.

TOPICS AND PROJECTS FOR FURTHER DISCUSSION

1. Have a report on the booklet *Does God Want You as a
   Minister of Education?* by Findley B. Edge (available
   from the Baptist Book Store).
2. Survey and report on the role of the wife of a church
   staff member. How can the wife of an overseas missionary
   assist in Christian service?

CHAPTER 5 OUTLINE

I. EVERY CHRISTIAN SHOULD ASK GOD, "WHERE?"

II. POSSIBILITIES IN CHURCH-RELATED MINISTRIES
   1. Overseas Missions
   2. Home Mission Opportunities
   3. Responding to Changing Circumstances

III. SACRIFICIAL SERVICE NEEDED
   1. Send Missionaries or Be Missionaries?
   2. The Urgent Need
   3. Modern Rivals of Christianity
   4. What Christians Have to Share

IV. KINDS OF WORKERS NEEDED

V. SERVING CHRIST EVERYWHERE
   1. Loving People to Christ
   2. Maintaining High Christian Standards
   3. Choosing the Right Way

VI. EXPERIENCE AS A GUIDE
   1. In the Home Church
   2. In Mission Work
   3. In Business and Professions

5

Finding a Place of Service

GOD has a plan, a purpose, and a task for every life. It is the responsibility of every Christian not to choose a vocation but rather to discover and to follow the vocation God has chosen for him. The right choice for each Christian is to do God's will.

I. EVERY CHRISTIAN SHOULD ASK GOD, "WHERE?"

Life belongs to God. All of Jesus' followers are called to make their vocations Christian and all are responsible to God for a life of service. God has equipped everyone to do something worth while. Having examined the fields where one may put his talents into service, the next step is to determine where God would have one to serve.

If, in the light of studies made thus far, one should conclude that God wants him to be a medical doctor, his problem then would be to learn from God where he should practice medicine. Will it be as a specialist in a big city, as a country doctor, or as a medical missionary on some foreign field?

Every Christian teacher is under obligation to determine whether God would have him teach at home or abroad, in a college or a seminary, or in the public schools. Whatever God's answer may be about the location of his service, the Christian is always under obligation to bear his witness and to give his testimony whereever he is.

It is expected that a young doctor who is going to a foreign mission field to serve as a physician would go in response to a divine call. But should not a Christian doctor in the United States likewise find his place of service in response to the direction and guidance of the Spirit of God?

Likewise, a schoolteacher who goes to a foreign mission field to teach should be led to such a place of service by a divine call. But is not God also concerned to have Christian schoolteachers elsewhere than on the mission fields? Does he not need Christian teachers, Christian nurses, Christian doctors, Christian builders, Christian businessmen, Christian administrators in the busy cities and in the remote rural areas of the United States?

The Christian therefore must discover not only *what* he is to do for God but also *where* he will serve.

If by inclination, talent, and training a Christian is best fitted to serve as a hospital administrator, he will want to examine the possibilities of engaging in this profession on a foreign mission field in one of the growing number of Baptist hospitals, or in one of the Baptist hospitals here in the United States. Opportunities for service may come in a private or a government hospital where one may make his contribution as a Christian administrator.

If one should feel that his talents and inclinations best fit him for the profession of law or for politics, his first question in deciding where he will set up his practice and what major interest he will follow in that practice must always be, How and where can I best serve and honor my Lord, Jesus Christ?

Similarly, in every other profession and business, the Christian's first concern should be that of finding how he can honor God in his profession. A petroleum geologist for a large oil company may have the opportunity of rendering an effective missionary ministry by his witness in the foreign land where he is sent by his company to engage in his profession. One employed by the Federal Department of State, or any other organization involving contact with peoples of other nations, will have the opportunity of bearing his Christian testimony while he performs the duties required by his position. Some men and women in military service have greatly aided the work of missionaries by their participation and support of Christian work in those lands. The predominant factor in determining one's vocation should always be how and where one can best serve one's Lord, rather than where one can make the most money, or where one can be most popular, most powerful, or most honored.

II. Possibilities in Church-related Ministries

1. *Overseas Missions*

Those who feel that God is calling them to be missionaries may engage in many different types of work.

"Missionary service overseas is an evangelistic witness which includes church development, Christian education, and medical services. If you become a missionary overseas, you may be the pastor of a church or the advisor to a group of churches. If your professional training leads you into science, you may become a missionary doctor. If you pursue literary studies, you may become a missionary teacher.

"The individual missionary's job differs from place to place around the world. But the missionary calling is always the same: to witness to God's power and love, to introduce others to Jesus Christ." [1]

Preachers are used on the foreign mission field largely as "general field missionaries advising a group of churches. Educational workers do much the same sort of thing on the mission field that educational workers in state Baptist and Southern Baptist Convention organizations do here in the United States. Missionaries serve as national Training Union secretaries, Royal Ambassador secretaries, as executives of publishing houses, as teachers in primary schools, high schools, colleges, and seminaries.

"Missionary service overseas is a demanding vocation. You will be called upon to learn a new, and perhaps difficult, language. You will have to adjust your thinking to new concepts of life, new patterns of activity. You will live away from the stimulation of many of the Christian friends and associations you now enjoy. If you have children, it is possible that you may have to teach them yourself when they reach school age; and you may have to face long periods of separation from them after they reach high school.

"Your consideration of missionary service overseas

[1] "Needed Overseas," a tract published by the Foreign Mission Board, Southern Baptist Convention, Richmond, Virginia.

is a quest to know God's will for your place of service in the world task of evangelization." [2]

2. Home Mission Opportunities

Dr. Courts Redford, executive secretary of the Home Mission Board of the Southern Baptist Convention, says: "God never calls a person to a service which he cannot render. You can succeed in the task to which the Lord has called you.

"Whether or not you receive an appointment by a mission board, you can render mission service. No mission board can make a missionary. All that a mission board can do is to take some of the missionaries whom God has called and channel their services where they will be most effective. Other God-called workers will serve effectively under other auspices." [3]

The Home Mission Board lists twenty-four types and areas of missionary service in the United States, Cuba, Panama and the Canal Zone, and Alaska. These include minority language groups living in the United States, service among the Indians, the deaf, migrants, Jews, and Negroes; work in good will centers, rescue homes, juvenile counseling, mountain missions, city missions, pioneer missions in the West and North, in evangelism, and service on the staff of the mission board offices.

3. Responding to Changing Circumstances

One's impression of a particular geographical location for Christian service should always be subservient to

[2] *Ibid.*
[3] "Whom Shall I Send?" a tract published by the Home Mission Board, Southern Baptist Convention, Atlanta, Georgia.

God's choice. One should be willing to be Christ's witness anywhere he leads.

When the Communists swept over China, driving out the Christian missionaries, the Southern Baptist Foreign Mission Board interpreted the situation as God's way of opening other doors for the Baptist missionary ministry. Faithful missionaries, so effectively serving in China, were reassigned to Japan, the Philippines, Formosa, Indonesia, Thailand, Singapore, Pakistan, and other areas of pressing need in the Orient.

This shifting of fields has often characterized missionary history. William Carey had planned to go to the islands of the South Pacific but God sent him to India to open a new chapter in mission history. Unable to enter India, Adoniram Judson entered Burma with the Baptist message. Luther Rice, expecting to serve in India, found his place of service in the United States arousing enthusiasm and concern among the scattered and unorganized Baptists.

Remember that "God so loved the world"—all of it, all parts of it. He who has saved and called his workers will place them where he needs them.

It is the Christian's responsibility not to tell God where to place him but earnestly to seek God's will. Those who keep the world in their hearts and in their prayers will be led to the places where God needs them most.

III. SACRIFICIAL SERVICE NEEDED

In some denominations it is expected that each member will give from one to two years as a missionary, going at his own expense to serve as a Christian witness either in the homeland or on some foreign mission field. Is this too much to expect of every Christian with a scriptural message to share with a lost world?

1. *Send Missionaries or Be Missionaries?*

The people of God are not those who send missionaries but those who *are* missionaries. To think of Christian witnessing, whether in the homeland or on a mission field, as the responsibility of a select few only is to misread Christ's command that every Christian is to be his witness.

Some of the Baptist young people who have served in summer mission work have remained on the field a year or more because of the desperate spiritual need there. Others have returned to secure the seminary preparation necessary for maximum usefulness in sharing the Christian message. Others have secured further technical training to go back to lift the level of health and learning through improved medical care, better agricultural methods, and better educational facilities.

2. *The Urgent Need*

A talented young college graduate was sent as a summer missionary to Alaska. So impressed was he by the urgent need that he arranged to remain in Alaska and help establish a Baptist church in a community north of the Arctic Circle.

Many young men who saw military service overseas were so impressed and burdened by the spiritual needs that they came back, secured the training needed, and returned to serve as missionaries.

Opportunities for Christian service abound in many

different vocations. Take a look at today's world. Multitudes are blighted with illiteracy, sickness, hunger, superstition, and false religions. Many are being led astray by false political philosophies that deny and defy Christian convictions. The underprivileged peoples of the earth, long exploited by more powerful nations, are now rising to demand their rights. They are eager to learn, to have a share in their own government, to own their own homes, and to occupy a place of respect and dignity in the eyes of the rest of the world.

3. *Modern Rivals of Christianity*

Communism promises the peoples of many countries the fufilment of their dreams. Non-Christian religions are experiencing a revival; Buddhism and the Moslem faith are competing actively for the loyalty of the hearts of the people. Surely, Christians have an unfinished task, a task that demands the very best that can be given.

The threat of materialism and secularism challenges Christian young people to proclaim an intelligent, confident faith in God.

4. *What Christians Have to Share*

To supply food and clothing, to share medical skill, equipment, and supplies; to provide educational opportunities; to encourage free governments; to share industrial know-how and agricultural skills will certainly give many opportunities of demonstrating Christian concern for those in other lands. The sharing of these must be accompanied by a sharing of the Christian gospel. Only the religion of love teaching brothers of every land to love one another even as they love Christ can bring lasting peace to the world.

Whether the Christian serves in his profession on a mission field or in the homeland; whether as a businessman, educator, physician, or political leader, it is his responsibility to make a worthy contribution to the winning of the whole world to faith in Jesus Christ. This must be the measure of every Christian's work. New discoveries in the fields of transportation and communication have made the world a neighborhood. It is the task of Christians to make the world a brotherhood.

The world is now so small that whatever happens anywhere in the world is soon known everywhere in the world. Unchristian behavior in business or professions here in America or overseas is soon proclaimed over the world. Every Christian everywhere is a part of the problem or a part of the answer in meeting world spiritual needs.

IV. KINDS OF WORKERS NEEDED

All kinds of workers are needed in the world mission of Christianity. Some will serve as volunteer workers in addition to their employment in some other profession, which will enable them to give free time to church-related work. Others will respond to God's call to give full time to church and denominational vocations.

With the rapid growth of Baptist churches and with the establishment of hundreds of new churches and missions each year, Southern Baptists need from fifteen hundred to two thousand men each year to enter the pastoral ministry. A similar number of men and women are needed in religious education and church music positions in the churches. One survey indicated an immediate need for over three thousand such workers. In association, state, home, and foreign mission fields, hundreds more will be needed each year. Professors, nurses, and hospital administrators are needed to meet the continuing demands of schools and hospitals operated by Southern Baptists.

On the mission fields and in the homeland workers with specialized skills are greatly needed. Social workers are needed to minister in the slum areas of the cities. Recreational workers are needed. Builders, electricians, painters, and craftsmen of many kinds are able to give their talents in building or remodeling structures for use in Christian mission service. On a few occasions the Foreign Mission Board has sent Christian contractors and builders overseas to spend some years on the mission fields supervising the construction of buildings.

V. SERVING CHRIST EVERYWHERE

1. *Loving People to Christ*

Whether a businessman, scientist, engineer, doctor, teacher, or a diplomat, whether serving in America or in some foreign land, one will be constantly in contact with people who desperately need to know what it means to be a Christian. If one's first concern is to honor Christ and to help others know him, he will enter every such relationship not with an attitude of superiority and condescension but with genuine love and concern. He will look upon other people not merely as potential customers or as so many hired hands to perform service for him but as people for whom Christ died, who need his Christian witness and to whom he may bring a message of love that can completely transform their lives.

A brilliant young student had announced his conviction that God was calling him to be a missionary to Africa. One of his university professors chided him about it saying, "With the promising future you have before you why do you want to throw your life away in the 'white man's graveyard' of Africa? Don't you realize you could do much better here at home?"

The young man replied: "I think it may be with missions as it is in building a great bridge over a river. There must be many foundation stones buried out of sight to carry the weight of the bridge. I am willing to be buried in an African grave if thereby I can help to build a bridge of Christian love to win those people to Christ."

2. *Maintaining High Christian Standards*

The Christian is under obligation to live by Christian standards wherever he may be. Whether on a job for his company, on vacation far away from home, away in school or in military service, the Christian will be firmly yet graciously and lovingly loyal to high Christian ideals.

3. *Choosing the Right Way*

The future of every person is only what he makes it. If he is willing to give God control, God is ready to give direction and supply the strength for him to live a victorious, useful, and fruitful life. In the United States one has the privilege of choosing his vocation. No dictatorial government determines what kind of a job one must perform. New inventions, new industries, new opportunities of service multiply the kinds of jobs that are available to young people. But the Christian exercises his privilege of choice by choosing to follow God's will in the matter of vocational service.

VI. EXPERIENCE AS A GUIDE

1. *In the Home Church*

In learning where God wants one to serve, experiences in the church from day to day will be a helpful guide. Experience as president of a Young People's union, as a teacher in the Sunday school, or as a leader in a missionary organization will help one to discover and develop leadership ability.

Experience in the church choirs, as a song leader in Training Union or Sunday school, as an accompanist for various church activities will help one to discover his interests and abilities as a church musician, which may lead to a life of service in this field.

As one takes an active part in all the work of his church he will doubtless have opportunity to meet outstanding Christian leaders from the mission fields and denominational agencies who come to visit the church. As one talks with them he can come to a better understanding of the various phases of Christian service in the denomination for both volunteer and vocational workers.

2. *In Mission Work*

Hundreds of Baptist young people are discovering God's place of service for their lives through the summer mission program sponsored by the Home Mission Board and the Student Department of the Sunday School

Board. Actual experience in conducting a Vacation Bible school, holding a revival meeting, organizing a mission Sunday school, teaching study courses, and other such activities will help one to find God's place for his life. Attendance at youth camps and assemblies will open many avenues of information about Christian service.

Some may have the opportunity to visit mission fields on a tour. Young men and women in military service often have opportunity to visit nations where mission work is needed.

3. *In Business and Professions*

Experience can be useful in helping those working in various businesses and professions to find the right place. The Christian "layman" will be concerned with such matters as health, educational opportunities for his family, and the future prospects of his business, but primarily will seek to know and to follow God's will. Experience in one community may indicate the wisdom of finding a more suitable location. He may deliberately locate in a community without a church there to bear his witness and lead in the organization of Baptist work.

Opportunities for Christian service are worldwide. Talents of many kinds can be used effectively. If one then is to follow Christ in his career, he will earnestly seek God's guidance in knowing where he is to serve.

TOPICS AND PROJECTS FOR FURTHER DISCUSSION

1. Report to the class the results of investigations, additional reading, and interviews relating to particular vocations.
2. Bring to the class some magazine article or recent book illustrating spiritual need.

CHAPTER 6 OUTLINE

I. THE IMPORTANCE OF PREPARATION
  1. Leadership Requires Preparation
  2. The Discipline of Study

II. TEMPTATIONS TO AVOID
  1. Paying Too Much for a Whistle
  2. Taking a Short Cut

III. WHAT PREPARATION IS NEEDED?
  1. Many Kinds of Preparation
  2. Educational Preparation
  3. Preparation in College and Professional Schools
  4. The Preparation of Experience

IV. HOW EXPENSIVE IS EDUCATION?

V. SELECTING A SCHOOL
  1. What Courses Are Offered?
  2. Cultural Opportunities
  3. Quality of Instruction
  4. Christian Environment
  5. Achievement Record of Graduates
  6. Faculty Strength
  7. Adequate Facilities

VI. SELECTING THE COURSES
  1. Wise Planning Avoids Expensive Changes
  2. Value of Mental Discipline
  3. Vocational Training

VII. PREPARATION CONTINUES
  1. In-service Training in Business and Professions
  2. Preparation and Life Adjustments
  3. Church Work Offers Continuing Preparation

6

Preparation for Service

"From section hand to railway president." "From messenger boy to bank president." America is still the land of opportunity. It is thrilling to know of young men and young women who have risen from poverty and obscurity to wealth and power as a result of ambition and diligent work. It can still happen in America!

I. The Importance of Preparation

1. *Leadership Requires Preparation*

Leaders being chosen today by business and industrial institutions are usually selected from those who have equipped themselves with thorough educational preparation.

One seriously handicaps his future when he fails to secure the best educational preparation available.

An examination of the employment procedures of local business and industrial institutions will doubtless reveal that in most cases their top executives were chosen from among those who had excellent preparation. Business firms conduct intensive recruiting campaigns in the colleges and universities seeking to find those with the brightest minds and the best academic records for places of leadership in their firms.

There are many factors influencing the trend toward more thorough educational preparation.

(1) *Specialists needed.*—Business affairs are increasingly complex. Technological processes involving great scientific understanding and skill make it necessary that those who direct these business and industrial processes be more thoroughly prepared for their jobs.

More and more, even the common laborer today must be an expert or a specialist of some kind.

A young woman in an office position may need not only to know how to use a typewriter and a filing cabinet, but also dictating equipment, duplicating equipment, and often complicated electronic machines that are in everyday use in an increasing number of offices.

In the factory men must be skilled in the operation of highly complex machinery. This is also often true in the building and construction trades. This is a day of specialization. On the farm, in the market place, in the factory, in the office as well as in the professional fields the young person without proper educational preparation faces an uncertain future.

(2) *Educational level is rising.*—More and more young people are going through high school and college so that the competition for positions of leadership has become strong. Only rarely will a person without educational preparation be able to compete effectively with those who have secured the necessary preparation.

2. The Discipline of Study

Preparation will not always be easy. It usually takes strict self-discipline to keep going when the way is difficult and discouraging. Yet courageous persistence will bring the satisfaction that comes with work well done and with knowledge that a coveted goal can now be more certainly achieved.

For young people who have the Christian concept of vocation, preparation must be considered an inevitable consequence of their sense of call. A call to serve is a call to get ready.

The Bible is filled with examples of preparation for effective service. When Christ called the first disciples he often took them with him for a period of training before commissioning them to do his work.

When Saul of Tarsus met the Lord on the Damascus road he found that God had a place of service for him, yet before he was ready to enter upon his great missionary ministry he spent some years in diligent preparation. After giving his testimony in Damascus, he went away into the desert for a period of three years of meditation and study. After a brief visit to Jerusalem, he returned to Tarsus for another period of preparation before Barnabas came to secure his assistance in the rapidly expanding work at Antioch. Paul was able to render effective service because he had made adequate preparation.

Effective service calls for thorough preparation.

II. Temptations to Avoid

It is not difficult nowadays for young people to secure lucrative employment even without the completion of high school training. The salaries offered may look attractive to those whose only acquaintance with the handling of money and the managing of their full support has been the decision involved in how to spend a weekly allowance.

1. *Paying Too Much for a Whistle*

Benjamin Franklin wrote about a boy who became eager to have a cheap whistle possessed by another boy. Having received a pocketful of coins as gifts from his family, he foolishly emptied his pockets into the hands of the owner of the whistle.

Many young people today are paying too much for a whistle!

An intense desire to get an automobile or some other coveted possession may lead some young people to forego further education in order to have immediately the things which seem to them at the time so tremendously important.

As with Esau who sold his birthright to Jacob for a bowl of thick soup, a perverted sense of values may lead to disastrous consequences in the future.

An objective study of the future possibilities of the jobs presently available to young people without adequate educational preparation will doubtless reveal that such jobs have a limited future. Unprepared individuals are destined to be limited in their range of vocational opportunities and in the prospect of any significant improvement in their economic position. In times of economic stress they are usually the first to be released and because of their lack of training they may find it difficult to get another job.

2. *Taking a Short Cut*

Another temptation to avoid is taking a short cut.

In many professions, of course, there are specific educational requirements which must be met before one is permitted to practice in that profession. A doctor must graduate from medical school and pass a stringent state examination before he will be permitted to practice. Similarly a lawyer must follow a course of very rigorous preparation in order to be able to pass the bar examination.

In the church-related vocations the standard of educational requirements is being raised constantly. Today approximately a third of the Southern Baptist pastors have a seminary degree. Another third have had some college or seminary training. The other third have had no college or seminary training. Every year, however, this educational pattern is changing as more and more churches are demanding well trained leaders as pastors, ministers of education, ministers of music, and as workers in other positions on the church staff.

Some denominations do not permit a man to serve as pastor unless he has college and seminary degrees. Among Southern Baptists, the standards of ordination are determined by the churches. Increasingly the churches are placing more emphasis upon the importance of adequate preparation.

Generally those who have better educational preparation are able to render more effective service. It is foolish to take an educational short cut. Often those who have entered church-related vocations without adequate preparation immediately see their need of such training and take steps to secure it so as to improve the quality of the work they do for the Lord.

Anyone who is willing to work for an education will be able to secure the training needed for effective service in the work God has called him to do.

Young people who have been tempted to quit school to go to work either because they feel the immediate need of having more money, or because they are dissatisfied with school work need carefully to count the cost over the next fifty year period of the productive life they will likely have before them. Remember that education is worth the effort it requires!

III. WHAT PREPARATION IS NEEDED

1. *Many Kinds of Preparation*

As has been indicated in previous chapters, there are many important factors in vocational success. Physical, emotional, social, spiritual, and intellectual qualifications are all important.

Likewise preparation in each of these areas is important. If one is to render fruitful and effective service he must be in good physical condition. Emotional problems can be solved and a healthy emotional attitude and pattern of life developed. The development of social graces and skill in dealing with people are vital in one's preparation for his vocation. Certainly the Christian will seek a continuing program of spiritual preparation.

2. *Educational Preparation*

One of the first concerns of a person who has made a vocational decision should be to secure the preparation required for his career. Each vocation demands a special kind of preparation whether one decides to become a farmer, a schoolteacher, businessman, industrial worker, housewife, missionary, pastor, educational worker, or enter any of the hundreds of vocations now open.

Fortunately, there are many sources of helpful information concerning educational preparation recommended for various vocations.

High schools and colleges usually have counselors who can advise concerning various vocations and the requisite educational preparation. It it is not locally available, send a request to the United States Office of Education, Washington, D. C., for a booklet entitled "Occupations, Professions, and Job Descriptions."

The best source of information concerning educational preparation available in Southern Baptist schools and colleges is the Education Commission, 127 Ninth Avenue, North, Nashville 3, Tennessee. This commission also publishes a number of free tracts concerning vocational preparation and a guidebook to Southern Baptist educational institutions entitled *Southern Baptist Campus Directory*. This directory gives a two page summary of each of the Southern Baptist educational institutions including location, curriculum, accreditation, student life, and basic costs, with a final section on student aid available in each institution.

After learning about the educational requirements of a particular vocation the next step is to find a school offering the necessary training.

3. *Preparation in College and Professional Schools*

American young people are going to college in increasing numbers. Limited facilities may make it difficult for all of those desiring to attend college to find one that has room for them.

Each individual will want to consider carefully the contribution that college training can make to his vocational career. For some vocations college training is a necessity, for others it is desirable, and for many vocations it is not necessary.

Those entering certain professions will need, in addition to their basic college preparation, further training in professional schools such as medical schools, law schools, schools of social work, and seminaries. These professional schools are highly specialized and require a well-rounded preparation as a prerequisite for entrance.

Graduate schools in medicine train their students in the many complex details involved in effective medical diagnosis and treatment. In a law school students study subjects specifically related to a law career. In a seminary, training is offered in those areas in which effective church-related vocational workers need specific preparation.

In most Southern Baptist seminaries, training is offered in three areas. Those who plan a pastoral ministry, either on the mission field or in the homeland, will be enrolled in the school of theology where they will study such subjects as Old and New Testament, biblical archeology, Christian ethics, speech, preaching, church administration, and religious education. The educational workers and other students planning for service in nonpastoral denominational positions generally enrol in the schools of religious education of the seminaries where they will receive training in Bible, theology, church history, church and educational administration, teaching, psychology, the philosophy of religious education, the history of religious education, evangelism, and age group studies. Courses in religious education will occupy approximately one-half to two-thirds of their total number of courses with the remainder of their work taken in theological studies and church music.

Those preparing for careers in church music should enrol in the school of church music of a seminary. In addition to music courses in theory, composition, conducting, musicology, and applied music fields they would take also a number of courses in the fields of theology and religious education.

4. *The Preparation of Experience*

Along with educational preparation, every vocation calls for the valuable preparation of experience.

Indeed, until an individual has demonstrated an ability to apply his intellectual preparation to the specific responsibilities of a particular task he is not adequately prepared.

(1) *The value of experience.*—Preparation will help to establish correct patterns so that experience does not perpetuate faulty or wasteful patterns of work. Not all practice makes perfect but correct practice does.

Every young person should if possible secure some experience in the field in which he is interested before making a final decision about his career. Such advance experience has many values. It will help the individual to decide in advance whether or not a career in that vocation would be satisfying and rewarding. Also, it will help him to determine what further educational preparation is needed. It will motivate that educational experience so that he will secure the greatest possible value from it.

Those with an interest in engineering or construction should seek part-time or summertime jobs to get some experience.

Those interested in church-related vocations should find places of service in their churches where they may render volunteer service. As they develop skill and maturity they may possibly secure part-time employment in churches or denominational institutions where they may later find permanent employment. The summer mission program promoted jointly by the Student Department of the Sunday School Board and the Home Mission Board gives excellent opportunities for preliminary experience in church-related vocations.

Filling places of responsible leadership in the church where one is a member is one of the best methods of preparation for fruitful Christian service. Larger opportunities usually come to those individuals who have been faithful in the smaller tasks. Such experience helps young people to understand themselves and to interpret God's call in the matter of a career or in a place of service in the church.

(2) *Southern Baptist Tentmakers.*—The Home Mission Board promotes a "Tentmaker" program. The "regulars" in this program are young people who have completed their schooling and desire to secure steady jobs in mission areas, usually in business or industry. While working at these jobs to pay their expenses they are able to give much needed service in the establishment and the strengthening of Baptist work in that area.

The "reserves" in the Tentmaker program are those students and others for whom secular work is sought during the summer in mission areas enabling the students to make money to continue their schooling while they use their free time in mission activities during the summer.

Further information about this program may be secured from the Home Mission Board of the Southern Baptist Convention, 161 Spring Street, N. W., Atlanta 3, Georgia. From the same source may be secured also information about the student summer mission program through which several hundred college and seminary students serve as missionaries on the various fields under the direction of regularly appointed home missionaries. The purpose of this program is to help young people who feel called to missionary service to discover their interests and aptitudes by actual participation in such work. The students render effective service in soul-winning, enlistment, training, and various other types of church and denominational service. As they return to their respective campuses and communities they arouse increased interest in missions on the part of other students and other church members. This program also gives the mission boards opportunity to discover the most capable workers.

IV. How Expensive Is Education?

Education may be expensive but it is worth what it costs. Young people in America are extremely fortunate, however, in having available to them a public school educational system that provides training through the twelfth grade without cost to the individual.

Higher education is provided in a large number of denominational, public, and private colleges, universities, and professional schools. The expenses of a student may vary widely from institution to institution and some individuals will spend more than others in a given institution.

Information in the *Southern Baptist Campus Directory*, which is published by the Education Commission, Nashville, Tennessee, indicates that in general the basic cost of a college education in Southern Baptist colleges will vary from $750 to $1500 for a nine month school term for those living on the campus. Expenses in state colleges and universities are usually not much less and, sometimes, considerably more than in Baptist schools, when all factors are considered.

It is recommended that interested individuals contact the various colleges in which they have a definite interest, asking for a catalogue and other information that would be helpful.

The expense of professional education in graduate schools of law, medicine, journalism, etc., is usually considerably greater than the cost of the basic college training. However, for those interested in church-related vocations, because of denominational support, graduate training in a Southern Baptist seminary is usually less expensive than college training.

Whatever the expense, it has been demonstrated in the lives of thousands of dedicated young people that those with keen minds, willing hands, and a persevering spirit can secure the necessary preparation.

Any Christian young person interested in going to college and seriously desiring to secure a college education should not give up until he has exhausted every possible resource. He should first check the catalogue of the college which he is interested in attending and find out about possible financial aid that is available to students there. From college officials and individuals in the college community, he can find out about the opportunities for earning at least a part of his expenses through part-time work.

Many churches are providing scholarships for capable and deserving young people from their memberships.

V. Selecting a School

What standards of measurement will an individual use in choosing the school in which he will secure further educational preparation beyond high school?

1. What Courses Are Offered?

The first factor will be the ability of the school to supply the specific educational preparation that his vocational career demands. For example, one desiring to become an automobile mechanic, a beauty operator, or a barber would want to seek out a school that would give the specific vocational training needed. Those planning a career in nursing will obviously need to find a suitable school of nursing.

2. Cultural Opportunities

The Christian who aspires to a place of leadership will be concerned not only with vocational preparation but also with cultural preparation in the liberal arts. This preparation can be secured best in a good college or university.

3. Quality of Instruction

The quality of training available should always be taken into consideration in the choice of a school. There are many measures of quality. One objective method is to determine whether or not the school is properly accredited. In transferring from one school to another, accredit-ation is usually required for the acceptance of the work done at full value. The director of admissions of any state university will advise as to whether work in another college in the state is acceptable at full value.

4. *Christian Environment*

Another important factor in selecting a school is envir-onment. This involves not only the way in which the courses are taught but also the general atmosphere and attitude of the faculty, staff, and students. A college education includes more than that which is learned in the classroom. The maturing of a strong Christian faith and the growing of deep Christian convictions are en-couraged by the environment that usually prevails on a Baptist college campus.

Students who decide to attend state or privately en-dowed colleges will be particularly concerned for the spiritual ministry supplied by the Baptist Student Union and the local Baptist churches, since they may not re-ceive any positive spiritual assistance from their class-room experiences. Baptist student work is organized on most college campuses in the South and West and new work is being established elsewhere as Southern Baptists become more numerous in other states.

Successive generations of students bear testimony to the fact that the Baptist Student Union has been one of the most helpful factors in their spiritual lives. Every young person entering college should immediately affil-iate with and participate in the activities of the Baptist Student Union. These activities include daily devotional services, Bible study, recreational activities, counseling, and mission services.

On many campuses there will be a full-time Baptist Student Union director ministering to the spiritual needs of the Baptist students on that campus. Many have attractive buildings called Baptist Student Centers to house their varied activities.

5. *Achievement Record of Graduates*

Another standard of measurement is the caliber and achievement record of graduates of the institution. If those attending the school in previous years have demonstrated ability in their chosen fields, one may safely invest his life in securing leadership training in such an institution. If former students experience difficulty when they transfer to other schools or when they engage in their chosen profession, it may mean that their educational preparation was inadequate.

6. *Faculty Strength*

A school can never be any better than its faculty. Discerning young people will seek those educational institutions where men and women of character and demonstrated ability are teaching. The influence of great Christian personalities on the lives of students usually outlasts the specific facts learned in the classroom.

7. *Adequate Facilities*

Despite the fact that many capable and successful leaders have been trained in schools with pitifully inadequate facilities, it is true that adequate physical facilities can make a real contribution to the total educational experience. Such facilities will include an adequate library, classroom space, administrative offices, service facilities, recreational facilities, and dormitory and apartment space. Such information is available in *Lovejoy's College Guide,* by Clarence E. Lovejoy.

Wherever possible, a young person should visit the campus of the school in which he is interested.

VI. SELECTING THE COURSES

It is important not only to make a wise choice of a school but also to make a wise choice of courses within that school. Many colleges, universities, and even some professional schools are much like a big cafeteria with a wide variety of choices available to the amazed, eager, and often confused students.

1. *Wise Planning Avoids Expensive Changes*

A careless selection of courses and of college majors often results in expensive changes requiring additional hours of work when one later carefully determines the educational preparation needed for his vocation.

2. *Value of Mental Discipline*

The student will be wise not to be governed by the courses that are most popular or which require the least work, but rather will choose those in which he will secure the kind of training that will give him the best possible preparation for a lifetime of useful service. College and professional school preparation should provide a rigid mental discipline that will encourage the most diligent preparation of the individual.

3. *Vocational Training*

Those going to college who plan to do graduate study in a professional school should secure from the graduate school specific recommendations concerning the undergraduate courses to be taken in college.

Those in college who are called to some church-related vocation should plan to secure a broad liberal arts education. They should learn to speak and write English correctly. Such students should be acquainted with the historic development of modern civilization. They should be acquainted with the basic principles of good physical and mental health. They should be able to live happily with their family and community groups. They should have an appreciation for great literature, music, and the other fine arts. They should be acquainted with the scientific method as well as the major systems of philosophy. Certainly they should know the essentials of the Bible and the Christian faith.

Upon this foundation the student interested in church-related vocations should plan his graduate seminary training so that he will receive specialized preparation in biblical, theological, historical, and practical fields.

Information about recommended courses of study in college for those who plan to attend a seminary may be secured from any of the Southern Baptist seminaries.

VII. PREPARATION CONTINUES

1. *In-service Training in Business and Professions*

Men who are going to the top in business and industry are those who continue their preparation. Some business enterprises send young executives to universities, institutes, and in other ways seek to provide for them a continuing stimulus to mental growth and cultural development. An important part of the program of most conventions is time given to in-service training for the business or profession involved.

Business and industry have well-organized programs of "in-service" training. Automobile and appliance manufacturers conduct "service clinics" for the mechanics trained to service their products. Executives gather to discuss more effective techniques in manufacturing, marketing, public relations, and advertising.

Medical doctors profit by professional discussions in their various local, state, and medical associations.

Several of the seminaries conduct annual conferences for pastors, educational workers, and church musicians, providing opportunity for those who have been serving in these positions in the churches to return to the campus for refresher courses, lectures, discussions, and demonstrations of new methods, materials, and techniques in their chosen fields.

2. Preparation and Life Adjustments

Sometimes circumstances change so that it becomes necessary for an individual to make a new start in his lifework. An accident or failing health may make it impossible for him to continue in his present position. Often such an individual by additional preparation is able to find a happy and useful place of service. One who holds to Christian concepts and ideals of vocation can adjust without frustration or unhappiness when inevitable changes come.

Continuing preparation involves not only vocational training but also preparation for effective functioning in the home, church, and community. With maturity and marriage there come the manifold problems of parenthood and child guidance for which young people may have little preparation.

Duties as a citizen in the community may call for the individual to prepare for specific responsibilities in the political life of his community. Every Christian should be a good citizen.

Additional preparation is called for as one takes his place of responsibility in his church. Opportunities for service as a Sunday school teacher, Training Union leader, missionary education counselor, deacon, or other such position should be a summons to careful preparation for the specific responsibility involved in effective functioning in this new role.

3. *Church Work Offers Continuing Preparation*

For such continuing preparation, the various church organizations have a well-planned program of study. Over two hundred books are now included in the various training courses promoted by the Sunday School, Training Union, and Church Music Departments, Woman's Missionary Union, and Baptist Brotherhood.

TOPICS FOR DISCUSSION

1. What kind of preparation is needed for success in the five most common vocations in your community?
2. What are the advantages of attending a Baptist college?
3. What opportunities for training in Christian service have been offered in your church in the past twelve months?

CHAPTER 7 OUTLINE

I. MAKE A GOOD BEGINNING ON THE JOB

II. MAINTAIN HEALTHY EMOTIONAL ATTITUDES
   1. Ambition, Right or Wrong?
   2. Christ Controls
   3. Attitude Toward Others
   4. Self-testing Exercise

III. CONTINUE SPIRITUAL DEVELOPMENT
   1. Make Time for Prayer
   2. Development Comes Through Service

IV. USE TIME RIGHTLY
   1. A Nation of Clock Watchers
   2. How to Use Time Properly

V. FACE DIFFICULTIES REALISTICALLY
   1. Family Pressures
   2. Social Pressures
   3. When and Whom to Marry
   4. The High Cost of Living

7

Getting a Good Start

GEORGE was a fine young man from a rural community. In Training Union he had studied about the importance of making every vocation Christian and had prayed diligently that God would lead him in finding his vocation. He had come to feel that the place for his life was a county agricultural agent. He had gone to college to secure the required training and had taken an active part in the work of the Baptist Student Union on the campus. Before graduating he had been offered and had accepted a position as county agent in his home state.

Realizing that the first few days in a new position are important, he was apprehensive about the kind of impression he would make upon those working with him. He was anxious to make a success in his new position. He looked forward to bringing his prayermate from B.S.U. days in college to the community as his bride. He was anxious to have a home of his own with a beautiful lawn and a convenient garden. These were his dreams as he started out in his new job. How can such dreams be realized? What are the factors that will help George to make a good start in his vocation and that will help millions of other young people like him to get off to a good start?

I. MAKE A GOOD BEGINNING ON THE JOB

To make a good start on any job, it is important to find out what is expected and to learn the approved procedure for performing each task. Sometimes the beginner will have a supervisor or an administrator who can give great help to him at this point.

In practically every business, industry, and profession, there are certain rules and practices that should be observed. Few such rules are made without good reason. Some are for the purpose of making an organization more harmonious and to avoid friction among employees. Some rules are for the protection of the worker; others are to encourage improved performance. The wise beginner will recognize that such rules can help him in his advancement.

II. MAINTAIN HEALTHY EMOTIONAL ATTITUDES

One of the major factors affecting an individual's success is his emotional attitude. The reason why some individuals of great ability accomplish little in life and others with mediocre ability make remarkable achievements is to be found in their emotional attitudes. Success or failure in any vocation will be largely determined by one's attitude toward his work.

1. *Ambition, Right or Wrong?*

Ambition can be either good or bad depending upon the motive behind it. A selfish motive will engender selfish ambition which can never be right for a Christian. But with proper Christian motivation ambition can become a driving power toward achievement. Those who look upon their initial employment as merely a stepping-stone to something more lucrative or to greater social status and prestige have the wrong motive. When young people enter upon their work with the feeling that they have found God's place and continue to serve faithfully until God gives some clear guidance that they are to serve elsewhere, they find that their work is both satisfying to themselves and to their employers.

If the young Christian knows that he is called of God to serve him in some vocation as God may direct, then his lifework is dedicated to the carrying out of God's will. His ambition then becomes doing the best he can to make God's will prevail in the world. The Christian will want to succeed in his profession or business in order that he may make his best contribution to his fellow men.

God wants every Christian to succeed to the very limit of his divinely given potentiality in the work that God has called him to do.

The life of the apostle Paul was dominated by a driving zeal to know Christ and to share Christ with the world. His ambition spurred him to devoted and single-minded service for Christ. He wrote to his Philippian friends: "Yet, my brothers, I do not consider myself to have 'arrived,' spiritually, nor do I consider myself already perfect. But I keep going on, grasping ever more firmly that purpose for which Christ grasped me. My brothers, I do not consider myself to have fully grasped it even now. But I do concentrate on this: I leave the past behind and with hands outstretched to whatever lies ahead I go straight for the goal—my reward the honour of being called by God in Christ" (Phil. 3:12–14 Phillips).

Such an ambition should be the spur for action in

every dedicated Christian life, persistently encouraging
God's workman to wait for God to reveal his purposes.
Such a Christian will not want to run ahead of his Lord
but will wait patiently for divine direction in determining where he should serve and what tasks he should perform.

The Christian will conduct his life not with selfish motives but always with regard to the needs and the rights
of others. Worthy ends demand worthy means for their
achievement. One is never justified in doing evil in order
that good may come. No right ambition will ever justify
a wrong course in its accomplishment.

2. Christ Controls

The lifework that is best for each Christian is the one
that brings him to the place of highest usefulness in
achieving Christ's purposes for the world. Many different
vocations are needed to keep civilization functioning
smoothly. God will call some individuals to church-
related vocations. He will call others to serve him in
other ways. All are equally responsible to the control
of Christ.

The Christian gets a good start in his career by giving
Christ priority and by recognizing that obedient lives are
always lived in loyalty and obedience to the command
and the will of Christ. Christ must come first. His slight-
est wish must be the Christian's supreme command. Any
honorable profession, trade, or business becomes a means
of worthy service whenever Christian men and women,
whether doctors or nurses, engineers or teachers, businessmen or housewives, serve God in their vocations.
Christ needs Christians to serve in all of these vocations,

even as he needs others to serve him in the pulpits and church offices.

The life of every Christian is a sacred trust from God. The division of life into sacred and secular is not based upon the Scriptures. The whole life of every Christian should be completely dedicated to the service of God, whatever vocation God directs him to enter. This means that every Christian will perform each task as a work done for the Lord. No Christian, whatever his vocation may be, should ever do careless work. A Christian workman should be a better workman than those about him who are not Christians. His convictions should be demonstrated in the way in which he carries on his daily work. To be a poor workman is to discredit one's faith and to dishonor his Lord.

Young people will recognize that different occupations offer different types of opportunities for Christian service, but the Christian young person will let God determine where his life shall be invested. Then he can know that whatever vocation he may be following he will be doing the will of God.

3. *Attitude Toward Others*

If one is to honor Christ in his career, it is tremendously important that he learn how to work with people. Academically brilliant students have failed in life because of their inability to get along with people. Honesty, dependability, enthusiasm, and co-operation are as important as education, experience, and technical skill. Many employers place personality first on their list of considerations in selecting employees. Personnel managers and business administrators report that employees with intelligence, initiative, ability, and good health are often seriously handicapped because of indifference or an unco-operative attitude.

Christian young people should begin every job with a determination to get along harmoniously with employers, fellow workers, and others in the community. They should meet each task that is placed before them with interest, confidence, and a desire to learn. They should not complain about the difficulties of their positions, but should look for ways of doing their work better.

One can get a good start by winning the friendship and the respect of the people who work around him, by earning a good reputation for doing his job well, by being slow to criticize but always eager to find a better way, and by demonstrating loyalty to his work and to those who head the organization of which he is a part.

One should not assume that because he has finished college or some specialized professional training he knows all that can be learned about the job. The wise young person will continue to study so that he may not only do his job well but also be prepared for greater opportunities of service. He will continue to read everything that will help him to do a better job. Magazines, books, and journals dealing with careers in practically every field are available. At conferences and conventions one can learn about others who are successfully performing difficult tasks in his type of work.

Aspiring young people will seek opportunities to talk with successful people who hold positions similar to theirs. They will ask them questions about problems that they have encountered. They will always be alert for improved methods, materials, and procedures.

Any young man or woman who expects to interpret Christ to others is under obligation to become the kind of a person that attracts others to Christ and thus to his way of life.

4. *Self-testing Exercise*

Am I concerned about the kind of an impression I give to people?........	Yes.........No.........
Am I genuinely interested in other people and their needs?............	Yes.........No.........
Do I seek to be co-operative?........	Yes.........No.........
Am I able to get along with my classmates, teachers, or fellow workers?	Yes.........No.........
Do I faithfully obey and respect the laws of my country?..............	Yes.........No.........
Do I refrain from quarreling with my family?	Yes.........No.........

My emotional score Good......Poor......

An unwillingness to co-operate makes it difficult for the person to succeed. The mark of the Christian will be that of concern for his fellow men. Jesus said, "By this shall all men know that ye are my disciples, if ye have love one to another" (John 13:35).

A Christian will follow the rules of the game, seeking to perform effectively his particular function on the team, rather than insisting on being the star performer.

III. CONTINUE SPIRITUAL DEVELOPMENT

Regardless of one's career, his maximum usefulness as a Christian will greatly depend upon his continued spiritual development. Spiritual qualities do not develop by themselves. They must be cultivated continuously. Jesus frequently needed to go apart to communicate with God and renew his spiritual strength. How much more will his followers need such habits of daily personal devotion.

1. Make Time for Prayer

The busy activities of the world today leave little time for quiet devotional periods. If one is to maintain such devotional experiences, he must do so by deliberate and continued effort. Christian young people should begin right by setting aside some part of every day for a quiet time for Bible study, prayer, and meditation. As an engine cannot run without fuel, as bodies cannot be strong without food, so spiritual lives cannot possibly be strong and fruitful without continuing spiritual cultivation. Christians cannot be adequately equipped to give a radiant witness to the faith if they do not stay close to Jesus. God is ready to give all of the spiritual power that his followers have developed a capacity to receive and use.

Lack of spiritual power is not due to the limitations of God's resources but rather to failure to follow the right pathways to spiritual power. The surest route to Christian effectiveness is the way of prayer. To pray is the most powerful thing any Christian can do. One cannot do anything important or effective until he has prayed. After he has prayed he can do much more than he could possibly do without prayer. Prayer connects man's weakness with God's strength.

To get a good start in a career, make time for prayer. Just as one needs to pray to find God's will for his life in the matter of a career, so he will need earnest, persistent, believing prayer to know his will in every life decision.

Jesus felt that getting a good start in any endeavor required time in prayer with God. At every major crisis he spent much time with God in prayer. So Christian young people must make time for prayer if they would get a good start with Christ in their careers.

2. Development Comes Through Service

Physical exercise is absolutely essential to physical development. No athlete ever developed skill, co-ordination, and strength just by reading books about athletics. No musician ever developed as a great artist without patient and persevering practice. No doctor ever became a competent practitioner without actually treating patients. People learn to do by doing.

Spiritual development comes through Christian service. If one is to get off to a good start in a new career he ought to put at the top of his list of priorities the necessary plans for continuing his spiritual development.

Jim and Betty had just moved to a large western city where Jim had accepted a position with an oil company. Both had been active in the Baptist Student Union on the college campus. Both were eager to continue their spiritual growth through service in a church in their new community. On their first Sunday they joined one of the Baptist churches. Soon both were active workers in Sunday school, Training Union, and one of the choirs.

Faithfulness in service soon brought larger opportunities—as Brotherhood officer, deacon, Sunday school teacher, and department superintendent. Jim and Betty have the respect and appreciation of the entire community as wholesome Christians who are not ashamed of their convictions. Their home has been blessed with children. Jim's personality and dedicated talents have brought advancement in business. Betty's queenly character has made their home a blessing to all who know them. All would agree they have made a good start.

Russell and Ruth came to the community about the same time to work. They, too, had graduated from college and were eager to make a good beginning in the job Russell had accepted with a research organization. Russell had ambitions to "get to the top" as quickly as possible. Ruth had social ambitions and set about trying to make contacts that would bring friends among the most influential people.

When Russell's boss invited them over for a Sunday evening cocktail party he decided he should accept for fear of offending the man who could recommend his promotion.

Despite some vague intentions of getting into a church they soon found their week ends occupied with trips to the lake, Sunday evening parties, and other social engagements. The standards of moral and physical purity by which they had once lived were forsaken. The expenses of the life they attempted to live in order to keep up with their social companions soon seriously depleted their financial resources. Ruth decided to go to work and thus postpone the family they wanted. Her added income helped pay for the entertaining they now felt obligated to do.

Trouble was almost inevitable in such a situation and it was not long in coming. Ruth became infatuated with a young executive in the office where she worked. Russell moved on from social drinking to become a problem drinker. Their marriage was wrecked, their dreams vanished, their joy in life was lost. They continued to pay, year after year, the inevitable price of forsaking God to live for self.

IV. USE TIME RIGHTLY

The Christian will get a good start in his vocation by making the wisest possible use of his time. Paul urged the Ephesians, "Make the very most of your time, for these are evil days" (Eph. 5 : 16 Moffatt).

1. *A Nation of Clock Watchers*

Perhaps no nation has been more conscious of time than America. Powerful automobiles are built in order to get their owners quickly away from the intersections. People patronize the airlines increasingly because they save time for the traveler. Some people become frustrated and upset if their plane or train is late, or if they are held up in a traffic jam, or if for any reason they are delayed. Whatever their right hand finds to do, their left hand usually carries a watch on its wrist to check how long it takes to do it.

2. *How to Use Time Properly*

Everyone has the same amount of time. No favored individual has more than twenty-four hours in a day or more than sixty minutes in an hour. Dr. A. T. Robertson, long time professor at the Southern Baptist Theological Seminary, had little patience with students who failed to study. His caustic reply when a student pleaded lack of time to prepare an assignment was, "Brother, you have all the time there is."

The problem for the Christian is not that of spending time or killing time but of using time properly.

If one would learn how to use time properly, let him study the example of Jesus. As was true in so many areas of life, Jesus was a master in the art of using time wisely. Although he recognized that his earthly ministry would be brief, the Scriptures do not indicate that he dashed madly and feverishly about Palestine giving an impression to everyone that he was terribly busy and that he had little time to talk with people about their problems. Rather, it is recorded that he had time to sit down to talk with a sinful and troubled woman of Samaria. He spent long evening hours with an inquisitive Nicodemus. He had time to sit down with a repentant and shame-faced Peter to rekindle his love and to assign him his task. Jesus had work to do and he did it. "My Father worketh hitherto, and I work" (John 5 : 17). He urged upon all of his followers diligence in their service, for "the night cometh, when no man can work" (John 9 : 4).

V. FACE DIFFICULTIES REALISTICALLY

Unquestionably there are many difficulties facing a young person as he gets started in his vocation. If he is to get off to a good start, he must be willing to face these difficulties.

1. *Family Pressures*

Family pressures in the direction of certain vocations can be intense with young people. Despite the freedom enjoyed in the United States on the part of most young people in making their own vocational choices, it is true that the occupations of parents and the wishes of the parents are powerful factors influencing the vocational thinking of the children.

It is normal for parents to have a keen interest in the vocational interests of their children. Every parent, however, should recognize the privilege and the right that every young person has to follow the purpose of God for his vocation in the light of his aptitudes and interests.

2. Social Pressures

Some young people will be strongly influenced in their emotional attitudes toward their vocation by the attitudes of others about them. Some people think of certain occupations as respectable and others as not so respectable depending upon whether they are professional, "white collar," or vocations involving manual labor. Some young people have the mistaken notion that securing a college education will automatically bring success.

Young people should remember that the social prestige of any job is not nearly so important a factor in finding a vocation as one's aptitude and interest in the type of work involved. Of greatest importance is a sense of divine call.

3. When and Whom to Marry

The choice of a life companion is often bound up inextricably with one's vocational work. A young man planning to enter medicine may find that he is in love with a young woman who feels that she could never endure the schedule and the frustrations of a doctor's wife. A young woman who feels that she has been called of God to be a foreign missionary may find herself falling in love with a man who plans to be a college professor.

One young lady, trying to escape from God's call to the mission field, chose as her life companion a young architect. She admitted later that she thought that surely there would be no prospect of his ever going to the mission field. But God had a plan for that young man also. He led him from architecture to the ministry and from a successful pastorate to a place on the foreign mission field, after a once unwilling wife yielded her stubborn will to God's plan for her life.

The problem of early marriage is often a serious factor in vocational planning. In 1900, the average age for marriage for a man was twenty-six. On the average, he would have been out of school for a dozen years since the average age for leaving school in 1900 was fourteen. The average young man would thus have a record of twelve years of work and accumulations to show to his prospective bride and her parents that would demonstrate his ability to support a wife.

Today young people are getting married much earlier. Half of the American girls are married by their twentieth birthday. Today a young man may face at a very early age the multiple role of being husband, father, student, and worker. Serious adjustment problems often exist for young married women, over 50 per cent of whom are now working outside the home.

Young people ought to face these difficulties realistically and make their plans carefully and prayerfully in the light of all the factors involved.

If young marriages are to succeed, there needs to be a complete sharing of ideals and purposes and a willingness on the part of both members of the marriage to sacrifice in order to achieve the desired goals. The tragic record of marriage failures should warn against hasty and ill-considered marriages.

4. *The High Cost of Living*

Another real difficulty facing young people, particularly married young people, is the high cost of living. This may create a real problem when young couples attempt to start out on the same standard of living to which they have become accustomed in the homes of their parents. Easy credit and the pressure to "keep up with the Joneses" often lead young people to make unwise debts creating such pressures that it is difficult for them to give their best in the vocations they have so recently entered and in the building of Christian homes.

Young people starting out in a new job ought to study their financial circumstances carefully and budget their available income wisely.

TOPICS FOR DISCUSSION

1. Which of the following are the most important factors in making a good start on a new job: appearance, conversation, knowledge of the job, ability to get along with others, willingness to work?
2. Plan a weekly time schedule or time budget for a person beginning a job.
3. What are the most serious difficulties facing young people in your community?

CHAPTER 8 OUTLINE

I. WHAT IS SUCCESS
1. The Proper Measure of Success
2. Each Life Has Its Pattern
3. The Changing Verdicts of History
4. Essentials for Success

II. DARE TO DO THE DIFFICULT
1. Dangerous Opportunity
2. The Challenge of the Difficult
3. Counting the Cost

III. "ADD TO YOUR FAITH . . ."

IV. THE MARKS OF SUCCESS
1. Love
2. Obedience
3. Changed Lives
4. Fruit Bearing

V. THE REWARD OF FAITHFUL SERVICE
1. Faithful Service Brings Enlarged Opportunity
2. The Master Calls

8

How Christ Counts Success

EVERYONE wants to be successful, but not everyone is able to tell what it means to be a success.

I. WHAT IS SUCCESS?

1. *The Proper Measure of Success*

How shall success be measured? Is it to be by the amount of one's salary or the accumulation of vast material resources? Is it to be measured by one's fame and popularity in the community? By one's power over men, machines, or nature?

Is success to be measured by what an individual has accomplished, or by the kind of person one has become?

Who have been the successful individuals in history? Will the successful men of this generation be those who have accumulated the greatest wealth or those who have risen to the highest political or social positions? What is the true and lasting measure of real success?

One may be acquainted with some very rich individuals whom history will hardly account as being successful. Movie actors and television idols whose popularity is great for a few years will not likely be listed among the most successful people in history.

What is a good definition of success? Is success doing something bigger or better than it has ever done before? Is it reaching a goal or getting what you are going after in life? Is success overcoming the obstacles that have hindered one's path to achievement? Does leaving the world a more beautiful, happier, healthier, richer place than one found it mean that one has been successful? Is success being able to make the best grades, being elected to the highest offices, playing the most important roles? As a Christian, what must be the measure of genuine success? This is a question which every Christian should ponder.

It is said that when Napoleon was marching from victory to victory in Europe, his aged mother kept asking, "Will it last? Will it last?" The answer to her question was given at Waterloo. It was written at St. Helena where Napoleon, during his exile at Longwood, wrote: "You speak of conquerors; but of what value are our conquests? Alexander, Caesar, Charlemagne, and I have founded empires. But on what? On force! Jesus alone founded his empire on love, and, at this hour, millions of men would die for him. I inspired multitudes . . . but now that I am here at St. Helena, chained to this rock, who fights and wins empires for me? What an abyss between my deep misery and the eternal reign of Christ! He is everywhere proclaimed, loved, and adored, and his sway is extending over all the earth." [1]

Napoleon had discovered the significance of real success.

[1] John S. C. Abbott, *The History of Napoleon Bonaparte* (4 Vols.) Volume I, p. 246.

2. *Each Life Has Its Pattern*

Jim was discouraged because he could not make the basketball team. He was awkward and clumsy and never seemed to be at the right place at the right time. Since basketball was a popular sport at his school he felt like a complete failure when the coach did not even let him join the squad and warm a bench.

One day the speech teacher invited him to try out for the debating team. He had never attempted anything of that nature but he decided to try it. To his great delight he found something he enjoyed tremendously and in which he did well.

There is a work for everyone, a particular place of service in which that individual can be eminently successful. Thomas Carlyle said, "Blessed is he who has found his work; let him ask no other blessedness."

3. *The Changing Verdicts of History*

Christopher Columbus, discoverer of the new world, was sent back to Spain in chains from his third voyage to the new world. After a fourth voyage, again with many difficulties, he returned to Spain where he died in poverty and neglect. Yet today his name is honored throughout the western hemisphere.

George Washington did not win all of his battles in the Revolutionary War. He carefully studied the situation, changed his plans with the changing circumstances, tried to profit by past mistakes, and out of frequent defeat and retreat managed ultimately to win the war.

Admiral Richard Byrd was recommended for discharge from the navy because of physical defects yet he stayed on to fly to both the North and South poles in his repeated efforts to explore the polar regions.

Nathaniel Hawthorne was a failure as a clerk in the Salem custom house. When he came home to announce sadly to his wife that he had lost his job, she encouraged him by saying, "Now you can write your book"—and he did!

Mark Twain and Sir Walter Scott were both literary successes but financial failures. Each lost all he had and incurred heavy debts. Rather than nurse their defeat in despair, each set about diligently to earn the funds to pay every obligation.

Babe Ruth struck out 1,330 times during his long career in baseball. But he is not remembered for his failures at bat. What the world remembers is that he hit 714 home runs.

Phillips Brooks was a tragic failure as a teacher at Harvard. Yet he afterward became one of America's greatest preachers.

Failure is not final! Success is possible for the Christian who seeks to find and to follow God's will. A Christian knows how to fail successfully!

Look at the life of Jesus. Would he be accounted a success? Is it true that large crowds followed him for awhile, until he began to lay down the rather difficult conditions of discipleship. He miraculously fed the hungry, cured the sick, raised the dead. He was discussed rather widely by the people of his day. Yet after a brief public ministry, he was taken out and nailed to a cross, a method of punishment reserved for the most despicable criminals. He lived out, in reality, the recipe he gave for greatness: "For whosoever will save his life shall lose it; but whosoever shall lose his life for my sake and the gospel's the same shall save it" (Mark 8 : 35).

A similar fate was experienced by many of Jesus' early followers. Stephen was stoned to death. James and Paul were beheaded. Paul wrote that for his love for Christ he would suffer the loss of all things that most men count dear. These Christians did not have enough influence to keep out of jail but their message changed the world.

What then must be the measure of success for the Christian? Certainly the Christian will not measure success by the presence or absence of material riches, earthly fame, or physical power. A Christian can be a success whether he is poor or rich, unknown or famous, an insignificant individual or the leader of great multitudes. These, either by their presence or absence, are not true measures of success.

One may well be a successful Christian without being aware of such an achievement.

For the Christian, ultimate success is to be measured by achieving God's will for his life.

> To know God's will is the greatest knowledge;
> To find God's will for one's life
>   is the greatest discovery; and
> To do God's will is the greatest achievement.
>   —GEORGE W. TRUETT

Is not this the best measure of success?

For Jesus, success was achieving the purpose for which God had sent him into the world. When he was tempted to turn aside from the cross, to take an easier way, he concluded that nothing other than his sacrificial death would suffice. He must go to the cross: "For this very cause I am come to this hour. Father, glorify thy name!" (John 12 : 28 Montgomery).

Jesus prayed and worked and lived until he could say to God, "I have finished the work which thou gavest me to do" (John 17:4).

4. Essentials for Success

There are two essentials for success in life. The first is to have a worth-while goal. The second is to keep on going until the goal has been reached.

Lincoln said: "I am not bound to win, but I am bound to be true. I am not bound to succeed, but I am bound to live up to what light I have. I must stand with anybody that stands right; stand with him while he is right, and part company with him when he goes wrong."

Success for the Christian means finding and fulfilling the divine purpose for which God placed him in the world. In such a vocation he will be able to bring to their highest usefulness all those talents with which he is divinely endowed. He will be truly successful as he finds satisfaction in his own heart, as he renders the greatest good to others, and as he lives out in his life the divine plan.

II. Dare to Do the Difficult

1. Dangerous Opportunity

Erma Paul Ferrari tells of a want ad that appeared some years ago in the London *News Chronicle* that read something like this: " 'Wanted: six men to take the place of one, a young Oxford man, who has just died at his post. Applicants must be willing to work without pay, eat Chinese food, dress Chinese style, and live a strenuous life in the rugged, lonely Kansu Corridor of the Mongolian and Tibetan Mountains, serving God and a needy people.'

"The picture so painted of life in this remote section of China was not rosy, for the head of the organization running the ad wanted no movie-inspired response from restless young men looking for adventure. And so he played up the stark truth, with no beguiling trimmings.

"Most of the readers of the *News Chronicle* would have been even more surprised had they learned of the replies which the ad evoked. Three hundred young men of Britain volunteered for the job. A careful screening proved them to be quite aware of what lay ahead of the successful applicants." [2]

2. The Challenge of the Difficult

Most people respond to the challenge of a big job. When Moses tried to persuade his brother-in-law Hobab to join the Israelites on their journey to the promised land he first said, "Come thou with us, and we will do thee good" (Num. 10 : 29). But that did not appeal to Hobab. Then Moses appealed to him to help with a hard job. "Thou knowest how we are to encamp in the wilderness, and thou mayest be to us instead of eyes" (Num. 10 : 31). Such a challenge to a difficult but worth-while task won his support.

God has tremendous tasks for his children today. Many have never accepted Christ and his way. Militant, godless

[2] Erma Paul Ferrari, *Careers for You* (New York: Abingdon, 1953), pp. 123-24.

communism, a revived Buddhism, a crusading Moham-
medanism, and a pervasive materialism are pitted
against Christian faith. The difficulties are tremendous,
the dangers real, the results often discouraging. Who
then will offer himself to be used of the Lord? God is
calling, "Whom shall I send, and who will go for us"
(Isa. 6 : 8). Who will answer, "Here am I; send me" (Isa.
6 : 8)?

3. *Counting the Cost*

It is not always easy to follow Jesus. He himself warned
impetuous would-be followers to sit down and carefully
count the cost of discipleship. The way is narrow and the
gate difficult to enter on the road that leads to the eternal
and abundant life.

When young Bill Borden graduated from Yale he could
have had many places of usefulness and honor. He chose
to invest his life in one of the earth's neediest places
where spiritual destitution was at its worst. With Paul he
was willing to suffer the loss of all things (Phil. 3 : 8) in
order to be "in Christ" and in Christ's service.

Albert Schweitzer was a successful musician and theo-
logian when he decided that he should enter some field
of service where he could give himself unselfishly in
meeting the needs of others. He resigned his professor-
ship, entered medical school, and upon graduation went
as a medical missionary to build and operate a hospital
in French Equatorial Africa. He explained his course of
action by saying, "It was the neediest place I could find."

Jack was a young research chemist. He was in charge
of testing a certain product in a research laboratory and
was responsible for writing up a report on the findings.

His immediate superior in the company had close connections with the officials of the company making the
product under examination. On several occasions he had
hinted that it would be to Jack's advantage to write up a
favorable report.

The tests revealed serious limitations in the product
and Jack so reported it. As a result his boss recommended
his dismissal on trumped up charges. As Jack talked to
his pastor about it, he said: "I cannot turn in a false
report. I need the job, but I won't sell my soul for any
job on earth."

Christian young people will dare to be different.

III. "Add to Your Faith . . ."

In 2 Peter 1 : 5–7 Christians are urged to "add to your
faith virtue; and to your virtue knowledge; and to knowledge temperance; and to temperance patience; and to
patience godliness; and to godliness brotherly kindness;
and to brotherly kindness charity."

Every Christian would do well to ask himself regularly,
What am I adding to my life? In preparation for the
twenty-fifth reunion of the graduating class of an eastern
university there was published a volume of statistics on
the lives and achievements of its members. Among other
interesting facts it was recorded that in twenty-five years
the class had gained three and a half tons in weight! One
wonders what the members of the class added besides
weight. If there were scales to measure moral and spiritual weight, what kind of a record would they reveal?

Parents and friends are always deeply grieved when it
is discovered that a baby is not growing and developing
normally, either physically or mentally. Yet there is

little alarm over the great host of professing Christians who have grown little, if any, since they accepted Christ.

IV. THE MARKS OF SUCCESS

Two college graduates were discussing the various members of the graduating class seeking to determine who in the five years since graduation had been the most successful. One of their classmates had organized a new insurance company and was independently wealthy with a spacious home and several new automobiles. They agreed that he should probably be high on the list.

Another of their classmates had gained renown as a nuclear physicist. The two quickly agreed that in this atomic age perhaps his success was as significant as any other in the class. Another of their class members had written a best seller which was being read by thousands. To be able to influence the minds of so many people led them to decide that certainly he was a candidate for honors in the success category.

As one turns to the New Testament, he finds an altogether different standard by which to determine success. What are the marks of success as they are found in the teachings of Jesus and the early Christian leaders?

1. *Love*

Man's supreme duty and privilege is to love. When asked what kind of commandment was greater in the law, Jesus replied, "Thou shalt love the Lord thy God with all thy heart, and with all thy soul, and with all thy mind, and with all thy strength: ... and the second is like, namely this, Thou shalt love thy neighbour as thyself" (Mark 12 : 30–31).

"He that loveth not knoweth not God; for God is love" (1 John 4:8).

However successful one may be at other points, if he lacks genuine Christian love in his heart he cannot be a success as a Christian.

2. *Obedience*

Obedience to Christ is a mark of success for every Christian. One can truly claim to be Christ's faithful disciple only when he does what Christ commands (John 15:14).

The Christian should live his life in complete obedience to the will of God. As God reveals the light along life's pathway, one should follow in that light one step at a time. Daily guidance should be followed by obedience. James 4:17 reminds the Christian, "To him that knoweth to do good, and doeth it not, to him it is sin." Jesus had nothing but contempt for those who professed to be religious but failed to perform. "Why call ye me Lord, Lord, and do not the things which I say?" (Luke 6:46). The Christian who allows his time and opportunities to be frittered away with idleness or meaningless endeavor while waiting for some great opportunity of service is sure to miss God's plan. Every Christian must do God's work every day as God reveals his will in every relationship of life.

3. *Changed Lives*

Successful Christians are new creatures in Christ. They may continue in the same vocations in which they were engaged before their conversion experience, but when Christ becomes Lord in their lives they will work on the farm, in the factory, in the shop, behind the counter, or behind the executive's desk with new attitudes, new goals, new purposes, and new procedures.

To be a successful Christian will demand that one break away from old, sinful patterns of thought and behavior.

A girl employed as a maid was asked how she knew that she was truly saved. She replied, "Because I no longer sweep the dirt under the rug."

4. *Fruit Bearing*

Jesus said, "By their fruits ye shall know them. Not every one that saith unto me Lord, Lord, shall enter into the kingdom of heaven; but he that doeth the will of my father which is in heaven" (Matt. 7 : 20–21).

The successful Christian will be a fruit-bearing Christian. His life will be marked by continuing witnessing, faithful worship, and diligent service. This fruitfulness comes as an abiding relationship with Jesus Christ. Jesus taught, "Abide in me, and I in you. As the branch cannot bear fruit of itself, except it abide in the vine; no more can ye, except ye abide in me. I am the vine, ye are the branches: He that abideth in me, and I in him, the same bringeth forth much fruit: for without me ye can do nothing" (John 15 : 4–5).

V. THE REWARD OF FAITHFUL SERVICE

1. *Faithful Service Brings Enlarged Opportunity*

Hear Christ's commendation of the faithful Christian, "Well done, thou good and faithful servant: thou hast been faithful over a few things, I will make thee ruler over many things: enter thou into the joy of thy Lord" (Matt. 25 : 21).

Not fame, nor wealth, but growth in character and in service rendered is a mark of Christian success.

As Paul came near the end of life's journey, he looked back upon his life spent in service for Christ. Faithfulness in service became for him the measure of his success. Because he had faithfully served his Lord he was able to say, "I have fought a good fight, I have finished my course, I have kept the faith: henceforth there is laid up for me a crown of righteousness, which the Lord, the righteous judge, shall give me at that day: and not to me only, but unto all them also that love his appearing" (2 Tim. 4 : 7–8).

The growing Christian not only finds joy in his work, but he also finds that he is increasingly able to do more for the Lord. Through continued evaluation of one's experience, through continuing study, prayer, and meditation, a faithful Christian will find that his life is one of growing usefulness and continually enlarged achievement in doing the will of God.

2. The Master Calls

"The Master is come, and calleth for thee" (John 11 : 28). As Jesus called for Mary and Martha so God speaks to young people today about their places in his service. Having become concerned about following Christ in their careers Christian youth should be eager now to find those places of service that he has for them. Life can bring no real deep peace and satisfaction to a Christian as long as he is outside the will of God. But in his will there is peace.

Earth offers no greater satisfaction than knowing that one's life is in the hands of God, in partnership with Jesus Christ, and that under the guidance of the Holy Spirit he is being used to shape lives and determine the destiny of souls by bringing friends to Jesus.

John the Baptist expressed the secret of success for the Christian when he said of Christ, "He must increase, but I must decrease" (John 3 : 30).

With this attitude and commitment every Christian may follow Christ in his career.

TOPICS FOR FURTHER DISCUSSION

1. Write out a statement of the Christian concept of vocation and discuss this idea with other Christians.
2. Make a list of some of the people in the church and community who are successful Christians. What are the characteristics of their lives that young Christians should emulate?

Bibliography

BOOKS

Bedford, James H. *Your Future Job*. Glendale: Society for Occupational Research, 1950. $3.50. (111s).

Browne, Benjamin P., Compiler. *Christian Journalism for Today*. Philadelphia: Judson Press, 1952. $3.50. (2j).

Coy, Harold. *Doctors and What They Do*. New York: Watts, 1956. $2.95. (48w).

Ely, Virginia S. *The Church Secretary*. Chicago: Moody Press, 1956. $3.00. (29m).

Ferrari, Erma Paul. *Careers for You*. Nashville: Abingdon Press, 1953. $2.00; pa. $1.00. (1a).

Kettring, Donald D. *Steps Toward a Singing Church*. Philadelphia: Westminster Press, 1948. $4.50. (8w).

Kitson, Harry Dexter. *I Find My Vocation*. New York: McGraw, 1947. $3.20. (6m).

Miller, Alexander. *Christian Faith and My Job*. New York: Association Press, 1946. $1.00. (18a).

Oates, Wayne E. *The Christian Pastor*. Philadelphia: Westminster Press, 1951. $3.00. (8w).

Shoemaker, Samuel M. *A Young Man's View of the Ministry*. Association Press: New York, 1951. $1.00. (18a).

Southard, Samuel. *Counseling for Church Vocations*. Nashville: Broadman Press, 1957. $2.00. (26b).

Smart, James D. *The Teaching Ministry of the Church*. Philadelphia: Westminster Press, 1954. $3.00. (8w).

Trueblood, Elton. *Your Other Vocation*. New York: Harper, 1952. $1.50. (9h).

Wolseley, Roland E. *Careers in Religious Journalism*. New York: Association Press, 1955. $2.50. (18a).

145

PAMPHLETS

Ackland Donald F. *Christ and My Future*. Nashville: Education Commission. 10¢ per copy. (Quantity prices upon request.)

Bushnell, Horace. *Every Man's Life a Plan of God*. Philadelphia: Westminster Press. (8w).

Chapman, Paul W. *Your Personality and Your Job*. Chicago: Science Research Associates. 50¢. (87s) 1947.

Clues to Your Career (a series of tracts on various vocations). Published by Education Commission, 127 Ninth Avenue, North, Nashville 3, Tennessee. 5¢ per copy.

Edge, Findley. *Does God Want You as a Minister of Education?* Nashville: Broadman Press, 1951. 25¢. (26b).

Frankel, A. H. *Handbook of Job Facts*. Chicago: Science Research Associates, 1950.

Kuder, Frederick & Paulson, Blanch B. *Discovering Your Real Interests*. Chicago: Science Associates, 1950. 50¢. (87s).

Nelson, John Oliver. *An Enlistment Manual for Church Vocations*. New York: Association Press, 1956. 10¢. (18a).

Nelson, John Oliver. *Every Occupation a Christian Calling*. New York: Association Press, 1956. 10¢. (18a).

Warner, W. Lloyd and Havighurst, Robert J. *Should You Go to College?* Chicago: Science Associates, 1948. 50¢. (87s).

TRACTS

Order the following free tracts from the Baptist Foreign Mission Board, Box 5148, Richmond, Virginia:
"Get Ready for a Real Job"
"Needed Overseas"

Order the following free tracts from the Baptist Home Mission Board, 161 Spring Street, N.W., Atlanta 3, Georgia:
"Whom Shall I Send?"
"Student Summer Mission Program of the Home Mission Board"

Order free tracts on various vocations from New York Life Insurance Company, 51 Madison Avenue, New York 10, New York.

Questions for Review and Examination

FOR INSTRUCTIONS concerning the examination and the requesting of awards, see Directions for the Teaching and the Study of This Book for Credit, page 153.

Chapter 1

1. What does a Christian have that belongs to God?
2. How may God make his will known to us?
3. Why should "full-time Christian service" describe every Christian's life?
4. What decisions should every Christian make with divine direction?

Chapter 2

5. Why is "full-time Christian service" not a satisfactory term to describe church-related vocations?
6. How can a job become a Christian vocation? What jobs could not be described as Christian vocations?
7. What did Jesus mean when he said, "If any man desire to be first, the same shall be last of all, and servant of all" (Mark 9:35)?
8. How did God call the following to change vocations: Moses, Samuel, Isaiah, Peter, Matthew, Paul?

Chapter 3

9. What are some effective means of measuring one's talents, interests, physical fitness, emotional stability, and intellectual capacity?

10. Describe the functions of a church vocational counseling committee.
11. List some helpful literature on vocational counseling and tell where it can be secured.
12. What does Jesus teach in Matthew 25:14–30 about the responsibility of each individual?

Chapter 4

13. Should a Christian enter a church-related vocation without a divine call?
14. What are the requirements for effective service in a church?
15. Describe briefly five different positions to which a Christian leader might be called in denominational work.
16. What should be a Christian's attitude toward changing vocations?

Chapter 5

17. What questions should each Christian ask God about his vocation?
18. How does Christian service overseas differ from that in the United States?
19. How many additional pastors do Southern Baptists need each year? How many ministers of religious education and ministers of music are needed now?
20. Should Christians send missionaries or be missionaries? Why?

Chapter 6

21. Why is adequate preparation increasingly important?
22. Name five different kinds of preparation needed. Indicate the importance of each if the person is to function effectively in his vocation.
23. What factors should be taken into consideration in selecting a college or professional school?
24. Name some values of continuing preparation.

Chapter 7

25. Under what circumstances is ambition proper for a Christian?
26. List the major means of continuing spiritual development.
27. Discuss briefly Jesus' use of time.
28. What major difficulties do young people face in making a good start in their vocations?

Chapter 8

29. What are some measures of success Christians would consider inadequate?
30. Name some "failures" who succeeded and indicate some reasons for their success.
31. Name and discuss briefly four marks of success for a Christian life.
32. What reward is promised the successful Christian?

Helps for the Teacher

IN TEACHING THIS BOOK, the teacher will be helping young people in one of the most important matters of life, that of following God's will for their lives vocationally. The teacher will have the opportunity of helping them to develop a Christian viewpoint on all work and to become acquainted with the opportunities of service in church-related vocations where there are so many pressing needs today.

I. BACKGROUND PREPARATION

1. In addition to the careful reading of this book, the teacher will want to become familiar with the other study course books in this series. They are:

For Juniors: *When I Grow Up*, Harvey Albright
For Intermediates: *Is This My Life?* Ruby Treadway
For Adults: *God Calls Me*, J. Winston Pearce

2. Make a collection of vocational guidance pamphlets dealing with various vocations and place them in the church library for use by the young people of the church. See the suggestions in the Bibliography.

Assignments may be made to class members to report on items of special interest.

3. Check through the literature from various Baptist agencies to find articles, lessons, and other information about the Christian concept of vocation and about opportunities of service in church-related vocations.

4. Write to the Church-related Vocations Counselor, Baptist Sunday School Board, 127 Ninth Avenue, North, Nash-

ville 3, Tennessee, for any tracts and other materials available on church-related vocations.

Purchase from the Education Commission of the Southern Baptist Convention, 127 Ninth Avenue, North, Nashville 3, Tennessee, a copy of the *Southern Baptist Campus Directory*, and other materials concerning education in Baptist colleges. (Price, $1.00)

5. Check with the Baptist Book Store on available films, filmstrips, etc., recommended for use in vocational counseling. Order any such materials well in advance and have a projector and projectionist ready when the materials are to be used.

6. Survey your community and area to discover those who are trained vocational counselors. They may be found in the larger high schools, the colleges, personnel departments in business or industry, etc. Find out if they would be willing to visit your church to discuss vocational counseling or to administer to the young people in the church some of the tests referred to in chapter 5 (an intelligence test, Kuder Preference Record Vocational Form C, Bernreuter Personality Inventory, etc.), and explain their value.

7. Arrange for a representative of a Baptist college to visit the church to discuss college preparation with interested young people.

8. Check with local high school officials about information that they may have concerning scholarships and other forms of student aid for those desiring college and professional training.

9. Discuss with the pastor the plans of the church for Youth Week, Dedicated Vocations Week, and Life Commitment Sunday. Give every organization in the church an opportunity to participate in presenting the needs of the world and the joy of responding to God's call.

II. Preparing to Teach

For the most effective teaching, one will need a lesson plan that will be drawn up in the light of the individual needs of those in the class.

Learn as much as possible about those likely to be in attendance. You may wish to prepare and distribute a questionnaire raising questions that will reveal their needs. The teacher will seek to determine what stages the members of the class have reached in finding their vocations. Decide whether the primary purpose of this course should be to help to give a Christian interpretation of the lifework they have already felt led of God to enter or whether it should help them to make the initial basic decision about their life vocation.

Check the church records to discover how many from the church have entered church-related vocations in past years. Learn, if possible, how many young people have made definite commitments to church-related vocations or have expressed an interest in such Christian service. Find out what is being offered in the public schools and by the church in the way of vocational counseling.

III. ENCOURAGE PARTICIPATION

1. Young people in the class will be much more interested when they have opportunity to participate in the class discussion. Topics for investigation and report, class projects, participation by visiting representatives of various professions and occupations, including several church-related vocations, will add interest to the class sessions.

2. Each member of the class may be encouraged to keep a notebook of occupational information. Individuals or groups making an intensive study of one particular vocation may share their material with other members of the group.

3. To those with special problems make assignments of material to read and report on briefly to the class. For example, someone may be asked to study and report on biblical accounts of God's calls: Moses (Exodus 3:1-10); Samuel (1 Sam. 3:1-4); Isaiah (Isa. 6:1-8), etc.

Brief book reports on such books as *Your Other Vocation,* by Elton Trueblood, will be beneficial.

Directions for the Teaching and the Study of This Book for Credit

I. Directions for the Teacher

1. Ten class periods of forty-five minutes each, or the equivalent, are required for the completion of this book for credit.

2. The teacher of the class will be given an award on the book if he requests it.

3. The teacher shall give a written examination covering the subject matter in the textbook, with at least one question or written assignment on each chapter, and the student shall make a minimum grade of 70 per cent. The written examination may take the form of assigned work to be done and written up between the class sessions, in the class sessions, or as a final written examination at the end of the course.

Exception: All who attend all of the class sessions; who read the book through by the close of the course; and who, in the judgment of the teacher, do the classwork satisfactorily may be exempted from taking the examination.

4. In the Graded Training Union Study Course, a seal for subject 3, The Christian Life, is granted to young people for the completion of this book.

Sunday school credit may be elected by the pupil. Application for Sunday school awards should be sent to the state Sunday school department and for Training Union awards to the state Training Union department. These departments will provide the forms for these applications. They should be made in duplicate and both copies sent.

II. Directions for the Student

1. *In Classwork*

(1) The pupil must attend at least six of the ten forty-five minute periods to be eligible to take the class examination.

153

(2) The pupil must certify that the textbook has been read. (In rare cases where pupils may find it impracticable to read the book before the completion of the classwork, the teacher may accept a promise to read the book carefully within the next two weeks.)

(3) The pupil must take a written examination, with at least one question or written assignment from each chapter, making a minimum grade of 70 per cent. (All who attend all of the class sessions; who read the book through by the close of the course; and who, in the judgment of the teacher, do satisfactory class-work may be exempted from taking the examination.)

2. In Individual Study by Correspondence

Those who for any reason wish to study the book without the guidance of a teacher will use one of the following methods:

(1) Write answers to the questions printed in the book, or

(2) Write a summary of each chapter or a development of the chapter outlines.

If the second method is used, the student will study the book and then with the open book write a summary of each chapter or a development of the chapter outlines.

In either case the student must read the book through.

Students may find profit in studying the text together, but where awards are requested, individual papers are required. Carbon copies or duplicates in any form cannot be accepted.

All written work done by such students on books for Sunday school credit should be sent to the state Sunday school secretary. All of such work done on books for Training Union credit should be sent to the state Training Union secretary.

III. INTERCHANGE OF CREDITS AND AWARDS ON COMPARABLE SUBJECTS

One award, either for Training Union or Sunday school, is granted for completing this book.

J. E. LAMBDIN
Secretary, Training Union Department
Baptist Sunday School Board

C. AUBREY HEARN
Director of the Study Course